You're in the Way

Breaking Free From Leadership Misconceptions

By Michael Hutchinson, MBA

Copyright Notice

Cover design by Michael Hutchinson, MBA.

With Gratitude

To my parents—the Northern lass and the canny Scot—thank you for your unwavering support and for instilling the foundations of the man I have become, and the one I continue to grow into. Your influence runs deeper than words can capture.

To my sisters, who have guided me in so many ways throughout my life. Thank you for the counsel and advice—both the good and the bad. I've taken those lessons and those conversations to heart, and they have been the steadying force that kept me on course.

To my son, thank you for becoming the brilliant and kind young man you are today. Thank you for forgiving my shortcomings as a father and for loving me deeply anyway. Never stop dreaming.

To my girlfriend, thank you for your incredible heart, your patience, and the way you take care of me while I push forward in both this book and my professional journey. Your support does not go unnoticed—it makes all of this possible.

To my friends, thank you for your belief in me and for the time you give so generously. You remind me that life is not meant to be all work—that laughter, connection, and shared moments matter just as much as any professional achievement.

And to the remarkable people I've met along the way—the thinkers, builders, and business minds who serve as my lighthouse. You have guided me toward better ideas, stronger systems, and a broader vision of what is truly possible.

This book is not mine alone. It is shaped by all of you.

Table of Contents

Introduction

The Fog and the Lighthouse

Have you ever felt like you're navigating through thick fog, struggling to see the path forward despite having great products, a capable team, and a solid market opportunity? You're not alone. Many business leaders share the frustration of marketing efforts that don't generate real sales, sales teams that struggle to close deals, and internal friction that constantly gets in the way.

But here's the hard truth: The problem may not be your team, your market, or your competition. It might be you.

Most leaders—whether they come from sales, marketing, operations, or finance—operate from a set of deeply ingrained, often flawed, beliefs about how growth happens. They assume that doubling the ad budget will automatically double the sales, or that hiring more salespeople guarantees higher revenue. They believe marketing is just about advertising and that the sales team should be able to close any deal if they "just try harder." They expect teams to work together seamlessly simply because they share the same goals.

These assumptions lead to outdated processes, siloed thinking, and knee-jerk decisions that waste resources, kill morale, and slow growth to a crawl.

This book is the lighthouse that will cut through the fog. It provides a clear roadmap for breaking free from these misconceptions and dismantling the barriers holding your business back. We'll explore why most businesses struggle with alignment, how communication gaps create dysfunction, and—most importantly—what you can do to get out of your own way and build a system that finally works.

What This Book Will Teach You

By the time you finish reading, you'll have a clear understanding of:

- Why the relationship between sales and marketing is so often broken—and the practical steps to fix it.
- The critical role leadership plays in either creating or preventing growth.
- How to identify and eliminate the leadership blind spots caused by ego.
- The real reason your marketing strategy isn't working and how to build one that delivers results.
- The essential structures and processes needed to truly unify your teams.
- How to craft a shared company message that resonates with both employees and customers.
- A framework for implementing and sustaining change without creating internal chaos.

Who This Book Is For

This book is for business owners, executives, and department heads who want to stop spinning their wheels and start seeing measurable growth. It's for leaders willing to challenge their own thinking, embrace new strategies, and build a company where sales and marketing work together—not against each other. If you're tired of wasted marketing budgets, underperforming sales teams, and internal friction that stifles progress, you're in the right place.

A Warning (and a Promise)

Consider this book your lighthouse, guiding you to question long-held beliefs about your company, your team, and yourself. But before we begin, ask yourself: Is my ego getting in the way? Is my need to be right clouding my judgment? Does the voice in your mind serve the company's greater good, or just your own sense of control?

Authentic leadership begins with the humility to challenge yourself first. At times, you might feel defensive or uncomfortable reading this. That's a good sign—it means you're on the verge of real growth. **In fact, somewhere within these pages, I've hidden a "secret" chapter—one that deals with the raw, personal truth of why we struggle. It's a chapter you won't find in the table of contents, but it is the one that might just change everything.**

Are you a know-it-all? I know I can be. On a recent visit to England to see my mum, we argued for three days about whether lettuce should be torn or cut. The "implications of our salad methodology," as I jokingly called it, became a point of stubborn pride. It was a pointless debate. The goal, after all, is a great salad, not being "right" about how to make it.

The same is true for leadership. Are you prioritizing the best possible outcome, or are you focused on proving yourself right? This book will challenge you to step back and ensure your decisions serve the greater good of your company. That challenge comes with the promise of meaningful growth and lasting success.

So, are you ready to clear the fog and let this lighthouse guide you?

Let's get started.

Ground ZERO

When Ego Crashes the Mental Boardroom

There’s a voice inside your head. You know the one—it’s always commenting, judging, and narrating your life like it’s auditioning for a documentary. Sometimes it’s a cheerleader: "You've got this!" Other times, it’s a nervous bodyguard whispering, "Don’t let them see you sweat," or worse, "You better look like you know everything, or they'll think you’re weak."

That voice? It’s your ego.

And in leadership, if left unchecked, it’s the uninvited guest who grabs the mic at every meeting, insists on being the smartest person in the room, and turns collaboration into a solo act.

The ego isn't malicious. It started as a psychological bodyguard. In our early days on a primitive landscape, the ego's job was simple: keep us alive. In the modern world, its role is to protect our identity and keep us from feeling emotionally exposed. It means well—bless its overprotective little heart.

But here's the problem: your ego can't differentiate between a genuine threat and professional vulnerability. When a colleague challenges your idea, the ego hears, "You're under attack!" It pumps its fists, rolls up its sleeves, and steps in front of the real you, snarling, "I've got this, boss." What begins as self-confidence quickly morphs into defensiveness, arrogance, and a need to control—traits that quietly sabotage leadership and erode trust.

Spotting the Saboteur: How to Recognize Ego in Action

Let's be clear: you are not your ego. But if you're unaware, it will drive the bus straight into a ditch labeled "Disconnection and Missed Opportunity."

The ego is subtle. It doesn't barge in waving a flag; it sneaks in through small thoughts and quiet justifications. You'll know it's at the wheel when:

- You feel personally attacked by neutral feedback.
- You mentally rehearse arguments before they even happen.
- You find it impossible to apologize without defending yourself.
- You crave credit more than you value connection.
- You avoid vulnerability like it's a contagious disease.

If any of that rings true, congratulations—you're human. The goal isn't to banish the ego, but to recognize its patterns so you can decide if it gets a vote. When the ego is in charge, it shows up in predictable ways:

- **It Blocks Listening.** When you're busy planning your comeback or defending your brilliance, you aren't listening—you're performing. Your team doesn't need a solo act; they need a leader who can truly hear them.
- **It Needs to Be Right.** Ever find it hard to abandon an idea, even when new information suggests you should? That's ego clinging to being *right* over being *effective.*
- **It Rejects Feedback.** Your ego interprets constructive criticism as personal betrayal. You find yourself explaining instead of evolving. But feedback isn't an insult; it's a gift-wrapped invitation to grow.
- **It Hoards Credit.** Great leaders shine the spotlight on others; the ego prefers to stand in it. It lies, telling you that sharing credit will make you invisible. Nothing builds loyalty faster than recognizing your team's brilliance.
- **It Micromanages.** "If you want it done right, do it yourself." That isn't the voice of excellence. That's the ego, terrified of losing control. True leadership doesn't cling—it trusts, delegates, and develops others.

Reclaiming Your Role: How to Lead Past the Ego

You don't need to silence the ego, you just need to stop letting it run the meeting. Here are five practical shifts to put you back in the driver's seat.

1. **Pause Before Reacting.** Your ego thrives on speed—quick judgments and fast rebuttals. Slow it down. A three-second breath or a sip of water creates enough space to respond with wisdom instead of ego. If needed, step away and tell your team you'll think it over.

2. **Name the Voice.** When your thoughts go into overdrive, label the ego like a cartoon character. "Ah, here's Defensive Dorris again, freaking out because someone else had a good idea." Humor disarms the ego. Naming it creates distance.
3. **Embrace 'I Don't Know.'** These are three of the most powerful words in leadership. Saying "I don't know" isn't a weakness—it's an open door for collaboration and honesty. It's also kryptonite to an ego that equates knowing with worth.
4. **Listen to Learn, Not to Win.** Practice listening like you expect to learn something, not just waiting for your turn to speak. Start meetings with shout-outs for others. Ask for help. Humility isn't about shrinking; it's about making space for the brilliance around you.
5. **Make Peace with Being Wrong.** You will be wrong. Often. Leaders who own their missteps build trust far faster than those who dodge accountability. See mistakes as data, not damage.

The Payoff: When You Step Back, Your Team Steps Up

When your decisions are no longer filtered through the need to prove yourself, you create a space where others can thrive. When your team feels safe, seen, and supported, they don't just do the work. They bring their best to it. This is what drives discretionary effort—the "above and beyond" energy that no job description can demand.

The ripple effect is profound:

- **Increased Innovation:** People offer bold ideas without fear of being dismissed.
- **Greater Ownership:** Your team steps up when they aren't being micromanaged.
- **Stronger Collaboration:** The atmosphere shifts from status to partnership.

- **Higher Morale:** People give more when they feel valued as partners in a shared mission.

Your leadership doesn't need to be the loudest voice in the room. It needs to create a space where every voice can rise.

Chapter Takeaway: Ego Awareness = Leadership Elevation

Your ego will always be your passenger; just don't let it drive. The key is learning to notice when it's grabbing for the wheel and intentionally choosing to lead from a place of service, curiosity, and trust.

Leadership Tip: Create an "Ego Check" Ritual

Before major decisions or difficult conversations, ask yourself these three questions:

1. Am I trying to be right, or am I trying to be effective?
2. Am I responding from a place of fear or a place of purpose?
3. What would this look like if I led with curiosity instead of control?

Write these on a sticky note. Save them on your phone. Keep them where they'll remind you that self-awareness isn't just a soft skill; it's an executive-level strategy.

Chapter 1

The Ghost in the Corner Office: Conquering Imposter Syndrome

You just landed the biggest client in your company's history. Your team is celebrating, champagne is being poured, and your boss is singing your praises. And all you can feel is a rising tide of sheer panic.

A cold whisper slithers into your thoughts: *"It was a fluke. The timing was just lucky. They don't know you were faking it the whole time. When are they going to figure out you don't actually know what you're doing?"*

In the first chapter, we met the Ego—the loud, obnoxious guest in the boardroom of your mind who shouts, "I am the greatest!" But every leader has another, quieter, and often more dangerous companion.

It's the Ghost in the Corner Office. It's Imposter Syndrome.

And while the Ego's arrogance can make you insufferable, the Ghost's whispers of self-doubt can paralyze you completely.

A Lesson in Humiliation

I learned about the Ghost early in my career. I was in my early 20s, had just moved to the United States, and had somehow landed a job teaching web design at a local college. The class was a mix of ages and backgrounds, and I was trying desperately to establish my credibility.

For their final project, one student, a kind woman a bit older than I was, decided to build a beautiful website dedicated to her love for her dogs. As I was reviewing it in front of the class, I clicked through the photo gallery and saw pictures of the dogs dressed in little sweaters and outfits.

Without thinking, a bit of unfiltered, snarky commentary slipped out. "I just think it's so ridiculous when people dress their dogs up like that," I said, intending it as a general, off-the-cuff remark.

A dead silence fell over the room. The student just looked at me and said quietly, "Those are my dogs."

The floor didn't just open up beneath me; the entire planet evaporated. In that single, horrifying moment, I felt every ounce of credibility I had tried to build as a young teacher vanish. And the Ghost was right there, whispering in my ear: *'See? You're a fraud. You're too young, too inexperienced, and too foolish to be in charge. You just proved it to everyone.'* The shame was overwhelming. My first instinct was to run, to hide, to never show my face in that classroom again.

But I had a choice. I could let the Ghost win, or I could own my mistake. I took a deep breath, looked the student in the eye, and apologized sincerely. I told her my comment was thoughtless and uncalled for. Then, I did what I should have done from the start: I focused on her excellent work. I complimented her on the clean code, the great layout, and how well she had applied every principle from the class—which was all true.

The lesson wasn't just "keep your personal opinions to yourself." It was much deeper. It was the realization that leadership isn't about being flawless; it's about what you do *after* you stumble. Owning my mistake and being genuinely accountable didn't make me look weaker; it made me more human. It was the first time I learned that authentic vulnerability is more powerful than pretending to be a perfect, all-knowing expert.

Banishing the Ghost: A Practical Toolkit

You don't banish a ghost with force; you do it by turning on the lights. Here are four "light switches" to flip when you feel the Ghost's chill.

1. Separate Fact from Feeling. The Ghost's power lies in making its fearful feelings seem like objective facts. Your job is to challenge those feelings with evidence.

- **The Exercise:** Grab a piece of paper and fold it in half. On the left side, write down the *feeling* the Ghost is giving you ("I'm not qualified for this job"). On the right side, write down every piece of objective *fact* that contradicts that feeling ("I have 10 years of experience," "I was promoted based on my performance," "I successfully completed X, Y, and Z projects"). Confronting the feeling with cold, hard evidence exposes it as a liar.

2. Learn to "Own" Your Wins. You have to train yourself to internalize your accomplishments.

- **Practice Saying "Thank You":** The next time someone compliments your work, resist the urge to deflect. Take a breath, look them in the eye, and simply say, "Thank you. I appreciate that." It will feel uncomfortable at first. Do it anyway.
- **Keep a "Brag File":** Create a folder in your email or a document on your computer. Every time you receive a positive email from a client, a note of thanks from your team, or achieve a significant milestone, save it. When the Ghost starts whispering, open the file and read the facts.

3. Dismantle the "Natural Leader" Myth. No one is born a CEO. Leadership is not a magical trait bestowed at birth; it is a set of skills that are learned and practiced. The confident leader you admire was once a nervous beginner, too. Frame your journey not as "faking it till you make it," but as "practicing it till you master it." This perspective turns every challenge into a learning opportunity, not a test you might fail.

4. Lead with Authentic Vulnerability. The Ghost tells you that admitting you don't know something is proof of your fraudulence. As my story shows, the opposite is true. Saying "I don't know the answer" or "I made a mistake" isn't a sign of weakness; it's a sign of immense confidence and builds trust with your team.

Chapter Takeaway

The Ghost in the Corner Office may never be fully evicted. Moments of self-doubt are part of the human condition, especially for those who push themselves to grow. But you don't have to let it haunt you. The goal isn't to never feel fear; it's to recognize the Ghost's whisper, acknowledge its presence, and then politely tell it to take a seat. You have leading to do.

Try This: Confront the Ghost with a 3-Step Reality Check

The next time you feel that cold whisper of self-doubt, don't let it spiral. Ground yourself by grabbing a notebook or opening a new note on your phone and running this simple, 3-step reality check.

Step 1: Write Down the Accusation. Give the Ghost a voice, but trap it on the page. Write down the exact feeling it's giving you in one simple sentence.

- *Example: "I'm not qualified to lead this project."*

Step 2: Write Down Three Pieces of Hard Evidence. Now, become a detective looking for facts. Your feelings are not facts. List three concrete, objective pieces of evidence that prove the accusation is false.

- *Rebutting "I'm not qualified...": Fact 1: "I was promoted into this role based on my past performance." Fact 2: "I have successfully managed three projects of similar scale." Fact 3: "My team lead told me last week that she trusts my direction."*

Step 3: Write a New, Factual Headline. Based on your evidence, write a new, more accurate headline for your situation.

- *Example: "I am qualified for this role and have a track record of success, even though it feels challenging right now."*

Chapter 2

Beyond Bossing: How to Actually Lead People

Early in my career, I led a small, talented team. And like many new managers, I thought my job as the "boss" was to be the master strategist, the one who knew exactly how everything should be done. I would map out the entire plan in my head and then hand out assignments like a quarterback calling a set play.

"You design it this way," I'd instruct. "You code it using this specific method." I was directing the *what* and the *how*, all meticulously focused on getting the precise outcome I had envisioned.

But I started to notice something. The work was good, but it wasn't *great*. It felt constrained. It was a perfect execution of *my* vision, but it lacked the creative spark of *their* brilliance.

So, I took a step back and did something that felt radical at the time: I stopped talking and started observing. I took a hard look at the incredible skills my team members actually possessed. One was a design wizard who understood user experience on a level I never could. Another was a process guru who could build efficient workflows in his sleep. I realized that in my effort to control the outcome, I was actively sidelining their greatest talents.

That was the 'aha' moment. My job wasn't to tell them *how* to do their jobs; it was to define the *destination* and then trust my expert crew to navigate the best way there.

The conversation shifted immediately. I stopped giving directions and started discussing outcomes. It went from "Build this specific thing for me" to "Here is the client's problem and the successful outcome we need to achieve. How do you all think we should solve it?"

The change was profound. By giving them the "why" instead of the "how," I unlocked their expertise. They started proposing solutions that were more elegant, more efficient, and more creative than anything I could have dictated. They didn't just follow my plan; they improved it, owned it, and elevated it.

That was the moment I stopped being just a boss and started learning how to be a leader. A boss gets compliance. A leader unlocks potential.

If you want to manage tasks, get a project management app. If you want to lead people, you have to do something much harder: you have to understand them.

Traditional leadership often fixates on authority, control, and being the one with all the answers. But real leadership—the kind that builds loyal, innovative, and high-performing teams—isn't about being in charge. It's about taking care of those in your charge. This approach has a name: **Servant Leadership**.

It's a philosophy built on a simple, revolutionary idea: a leader's primary role is to serve their team's needs, not the other way around. By focusing on empowering, developing, and supporting your people, you create an environment where everyone can do their best work. This chapter is your guide to putting that philosophy into action.

Pillar 1: Start with Who — Understand Your People

Effective leadership begins with knowing who you're leading. It's not just about their skills, but their personalities, motivations, and communication styles. Some people thrive on direct guidance; others need autonomy to fly. Some are driven by personal achievement; others are motivated by collaboration.

You can't lead a team of strangers. Get to know them.

- What are their career goals?
- What parts of their job do they love? What parts do they tolerate?
- How do they prefer to receive feedback?

Understanding this allows you to stop using a one-size-fits-all approach and start adapting your style to unlock each person's potential.

Pillar 2: The Empathy-Logic Balance

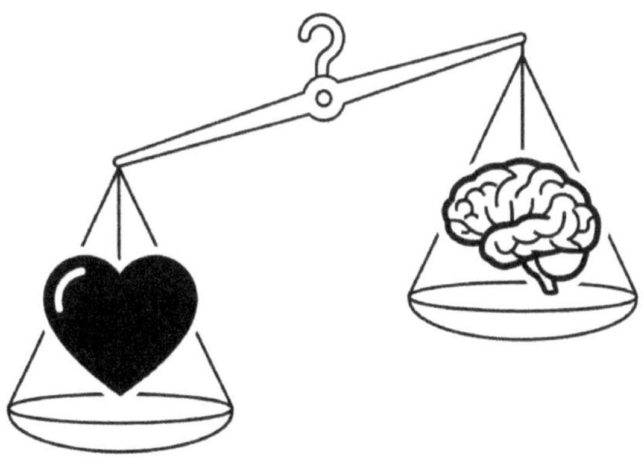

Empathy is your leadership superpower. It's the ability to understand and share the feelings of others, and it's the glue that builds trust. When your team members feel genuinely seen and heard, they become more engaged, motivated, and loyal.

However, empathy without logic can become a liability. If you're so afraid of hurting someone's feelings that you can't give honest feedback or make a tough but necessary decision, you aren't leading —you're people-pleasing.

The key is to balance empathy with objective, logical thinking.

- **Empathy asks:** "How is my team feeling about this tight deadline?"
- **Logic asks:** "What are the root causes of the delay, and what objective steps must we take to get back on track?"

A great leader uses both. When discussing a performance issue, you might say, "I understand you've had a lot on your plate lately, and I appreciate the effort you're putting in. Let's look at the project goals together and figure out a plan to meet our upcoming deadline." This approach validates their feelings while upholding accountability.

Pillar 3: Empower Through Action

Once you understand your team and have the right mindset, you empower them through consistent action. This is where servant leadership moves from idea to impact.

- **Provide the Right Tools and Get Rid of the Wrong Ones.** Ensure your team has the resources, training, and time they need to succeed. But just as importantly, be willing to ditch the things that hinder them. I find it deeply frustrating when management forces tools or processes on a team that are clunky and inefficient. Don't cling to a failing strategy just because you've invested in it. If it's not working, admit it and ask your team for a better path forward.

- **Encourage Ownership (and Get Out of the Way).** Nothing fosters commitment like ownership. Assign responsibility, set clear expectations, and then step back. Resist the urge to micromanage. Trust your team to deliver, and only offer feedback when it's truly needed. Remember: you don't know everything, and you can't do everything. Stop being a bottleneck.
- **Build Unshakeable Trust.** Trust is the currency of leadership. Build it by being transparent, keeping your word, and taking responsibility when things go wrong. Instead of assigning blame, gather the team to find a solution. This creates a safe environment where people feel secure enough to share ideas, admit mistakes, and collaborate openly.
- **Run Meetings That Serve, Not Steal.** Your team's time is their most valuable resource. Don't waste it on meetings that could have been an email. Have a clear agenda, stick to it, and keep it brief. A meeting should be a tool for progress, not a barrier to productivity.

Pillar 4: Lead the Charge on Change

The business world is constantly evolving, and so are the tools we use. Holding onto old methods just because they're familiar is a recipe for stagnation. A leader's job is to foster a culture that doesn't just tolerate change, but embraces it.

- **Challenge Your Own Assumptions.** Your preconceived notions about "how things should be done" can limit your team's potential. Be the first to question established norms. Ask, "Is this marketing strategy still effective, or are we just doing it because we always have?"
- **Create a Safe Space for New Ideas.** Creativity thrives when people aren't afraid to look silly. Encourage brainstorming where

all ideas are welcome. Foster an environment where your team feels empowered to question the status quo and propose innovative solutions.

- **Embrace Continuous Learning.** Actively commit to your own growth. Read widely, seek feedback, and share what you learn with your team. Host a monthly knowledge-sharing session or invest in professional development. When the leader models a commitment to learning, the whole team rises.

Chapter Takeaway

Effective leadership isn't a title; it's a series of conscious choices. It's choosing service over self, trust over control, and adaptability over tradition. By focusing on understanding your people, balancing empathy with logic, and empowering your team to act and innovate, you build a resilient, engaged, and highly effective organization.

Try This: Your New Delegation Script

The fastest way to shift from "boss" to "leader" is to change the way you delegate. The next time you assign a task, consciously use this simple, three-part script in your conversation.

The "Outcome, Not How-To" Frame

1. State the Desired Outcome and the "Why." Start by explaining the goal and why it matters.

- *Instead of:* "I need you to create a three-slide PowerPoint."
- *Try:* "We need to present our Q3 findings to the executive team so they can confidently approve our budget for next year. The 'why' here is building their confidence in our progress."

2. Clarify the Constraints and Resources. Define the boundaries and what's available to them.

- *Example:* "The only hard constraints are that the presentation needs to be under 10 minutes and must use the official company template. You have full access to the analytics dashboard and two hours of the design team's time if you need it."

3. Empower with an Open-Ended Question. This is the most important step. It transfers ownership and unlocks their expertise.

- *Instead of:* "Let me know when the PowerPoint is done."
- *Try:* "Based on that outcome, what do you think is the best way to tell this story?"

Chapter 3

The Lighthouse View: Seeing Your Business Through the Fog

Most leaders are so busy navigating the fog that they forget their most important job: to climb the lighthouse and see the entire coastline.

Day-to-day operations are a chaotic sea of urgent tasks, team issues, and immediate deadlines. This is the "ship level," and it's easy to get trapped there, reacting to the nearest wave. But when you're wrestling with the helm in a dense fog, you can't see the dangerous rocks ahead or the clear channel just a few degrees to port. You lose perspective.

The lighthouse view—a strategic, stationary perspective high above the churning waters—is not a luxury; it's a necessity. It's the only way to cut through the noise, spot hidden patterns, and ensure all the moving parts of your business are actually sailing in the same direction. This chapter is your guide to climbing the tower. We'll focus on three critical areas your lighthouse beam must illuminate: your structure, your offerings, and your culture.

Vantage Point 1: The Structure — The Foundation of Your Lighthouse

From the deck of the ship, your company can feel like a chaotic mess of ropes and sails. From the top of the lighthouse, you should be able to see its design. Understanding your company's structure is the first step to making it seaworthy.

- **Map Your Blueprint:** Start with a clear organizational chart. Who reports to whom? Where are the official lines of communication? This isn't just a bureaucratic exercise; it's about revealing where the structure is weak. If your marketing and sales teams are in separate wings of the lighthouse with no connecting staircase, you've just found a primary source of dysfunction.
- **Clarify Roles and Responsibilities:** A sound structure gives everyone a clear purpose. When crew members know precisely what they are responsible for and who to turn to for guidance, it eliminates confusion and encourages collaboration. Ambiguity is the storm that sinks ships.
- **Observe the Flow of Information:** How do different departments signal each other? Is communication clear and direct, or does a message have to be passed through multiple people, getting distorted along the way? A slow or broken flow of information is a symptom of a structural flaw that needs fixing.

Vantage Point 2: The Offerings — The Ships in the Water

You might feel you know your products and services intimately, but the lighthouse view reveals the full regatta—which ships are sailing swiftly, which are taking on water, and which are dead in the calm.

- **Assess Your Entire Fleet:** List every product and service you offer. Now, shine your light on the data. Which ships are bringing in the most treasure? Which are the most profitable? Which ones are draining resources with little return? You may discover that your flagship product is actually a financial drain, while a smaller, overlooked boat is the fastest in the fleet.
- **Listen to the Signals from Shore:** Your customers have the answers. Use feedback surveys, read online reviews, and talk to your sales and support teams on the docks. Are customers happy with the quality of your ships? Do they feel the price of passage is fair? Are there new features they are begging for? This data isn't just noise; it's a star chart for future navigation.
- **Analyze the Tides and Currents:** Look at sales data over time. Are there seasonal tides? Is the current of demand for a certain product growing stronger or weaker? This perspective allows you to move from reactive decision-making ("We're about to run aground!") to proactive strategy ("Let's prepare our fleet to catch the favorable tide in Q3").

Vantage Point 3: The Culture — The Sea and the Sky

Company culture is the invisible force that determines whether you sail on calm seas under clear skies or battle through a perpetual storm. From the ship, you only feel the waves. From the lighthouse, you can see the weather patterns forming.

- **Forecast the Weather:** You can't change the weather if you don't know it's coming. Use anonymous employee engagement surveys to get an honest forecast on job satisfaction, teamwork, and morale. If a storm is brewing, these surveys will help you pinpoint the *why* behind it. Is it a lack of recognition? Limited opportunities for advancement? Poor communication from the captain?

- **Identify Your True North:** Your company has a stated destination—the mission written on your maps. It also has a *true* heading—the behaviors that actually get rewarded. From your high vantage point, observe what it truly takes to get ahead in your company. Is it collaboration or mutiny? Innovation or just rowing faster? If your true north doesn't match your compass, you have a culture problem.
- **Create Safe Harbors:** Does your crew feel safe to speak up, share bold ideas, or admit mistakes without fear of being thrown overboard? A culture of fear makes everyone hide below deck, stifling innovation and honesty. Your actions are the beacon that signals whether the harbor is safe or not.

From Illumination to Action

The light from your tower is useless if it doesn't guide anyone. Once you have a clearer picture, your job is to use that light to guide your fleet.

- **Set Your Coordinates:** Use what you've learned to establish clear Key Performance Indicators (KPIs). Instead of a vague goal like "sail better," set a specific course: "Increase the speed of Ship X by 15% this quarter by rigging a new set of sails (a targeted digital marketing campaign)."
- **Share the View from the Top:** Don't keep this perspective to yourself. Share your findings and goals with your officers and the entire crew. When everyone understands the destination and sees how their work helps the fleet get there, you create alignment and a powerful sense of shared purpose.

- **Keep Watch and Adjust Course:** The sea is always changing. A lighthouse keeper's work is never done. Hold regular strategic reviews to assess your progress and be ready to adjust your course. In navigation, flexibility is strength.

Chapter Takeaway

Your role as a leader is to be the keeper of your organization's lighthouse. While you must spend time on the ships to understand the crew's challenges, your unique value lies in your ability to climb the tower, operate the light, and provide the perspective that allows the entire fleet to navigate the fog and reach its destination safely.

Try This: Your Weekly Lighthouse Scan

To make a high-level view a habit, block out 30 minutes on your calendar every Friday for your "Lighthouse Scan." In a notebook or a digital document, answer the following questions about the week that just passed.

Vantage Point 1: Your Structure

- Where did our team get stuck this week due to a clunky process or an unclear decision-maker?
- What is one communication gap I witnessed that I can help bridge next week?

Vantage Point 2: Your Offerings

- Based on this week's data and feedback, what is one thing we learned about what our customers *truly* value?
- Is there an "overlooked" product that showed surprising potential this week?

Vantage Point 3: Your Culture

- What was the dominant emotion of my team this week (e.g., Energized, stressed, focused)?
- Who on my team deserves a public shout-out next week for demonstrating one of our core values?

The Secret Chapter

The Mirror and the Maze

Somewhere along the way, we were sold a quiet, poisonous lie: **That who you are is separate from what you do.**

We treat personal growth as a luxury—a weekend retreat or a book on the nightstand—while professional growth is treated as survival. We optimize our calendars, chase KPIs, and hustle for outcomes, all while operating under the delusion that happiness is a trophy waiting for us at the finish line.

But have you noticed? Even when things improve on paper, the "hollow" feeling remains.

The Weight of Waiting

I learned this in the quiet, lonely spaces of a life that looked fine from the outside. Mainly, it looked like what I was supposed to do.

Shortly after moving to America, I was drowning in a sea of "shoulds." I was deeply homesick for the culture and familiar faces of England. My marriage was fraying at the edges. At work, I had become an expendable asset—valued for my output, but invisible as a person.

I had a job. I was paying the bills (barely). On the surface, I was doing exactly what society expects of an adult. I was showing up, I was grinding, and I was keeping the lights on. But internally, I was in a perpetual state of **waiting**.

- Waiting to feel settled.
- Waiting for my boss to notice my worth.
- Waiting for my circumstances to finally give me permission to be happy.

That was my mistake. I was treating my joy like a package that had been delayed in the mail, sitting on the porch, angry at the delivery driver. The shift happened when I realized: **Happiness isn't a delivery. It's a decision (every day).**

The Grocery Store Paradox

Choosing happiness is uncomfortable because it requires you to set down your favorite weapon: **Blame.**

It is so much easier to blame the toxic culture, the demanding spouse, the bad economy, or the relentless pressure. But looking outside of yourself for fulfillment is a dead end. No title, no salary, and no person can consistently carry the weight of your internal stability.

Think about how you shop at the grocery store. You don't wander the aisles in a trance, hoping the right food falls into your cart.

- You know what you like.
- You know what makes you feel nourished.
- You know which treats are worth the indulgence.

You choose.

Life is the same aisle. You already know the habits that drain you. You know the attitudes that act like an anchor. You know the patterns that keep you looping in the same cycles. You aren't confused; you're just hesitant to make a different selection, or you think it's beyond your control.

Your Professional Ceiling is a Personal Foundation

Here is the truth most leadership books are too polite to mention: **You do not outgrow your character flaws just because you got a promotion.**

Leadership is not a role; it's a pattern. And patterns follow you into every boardroom and Zoom call you join.

- If you can't set boundaries at home, you'll be a doormat for your clients.
- If you avoid "the talk" with your partner, you'll avoid the "hard conversation" with your underperformer.
- If you don't trust yourself, you will outsource your soul to anyone who offers validation.

We try to compartmentalize, but the cracks in the foundation eventually show in the penthouse.

Happiness as Strategy

There's a persistent myth that "working on yourself" is soft. In reality, emotional groundedness is a **competitive advantage**.

When I stopped waiting for my environment to fix my mood, my leadership transformed. I became less reactive and more intentional. I stopped being desperate for approval, which ironically made me more deserving of it. I wasn't pushing harder; I just stopped fighting myself.

> **The most important work you will ever do won't show up on a résumé. It's the work of catching yourself before you default to an old, misguided version of you.**

The Evolution Without an End

The most vital thing to understand is this: **There is no finish line.**

The pursuit of personal happiness and growth isn't a mountain you climb once, so you can sit at the top forever. Life is always moving. Your circumstances will shift, your industry will change, and new challenges will arrive that you didn't see coming.

Evolution is continuous. You don't "reach" growth; you inhabit it. The important part—the only part you truly possess—is your control over your choices. You get to decide, every single morning, to evolve as a person. You choose to adapt, to learn, and to refuse to let the world dictate your internal state.

The First Step (Is Inward)

I didn't flip a switch and become enlightened overnight. It started with one difficult realization: **I had to stop outsourcing my happiness.**

Your first step isn't a new job or a new city. It's a new perspective. You aren't "in the way" because you lack a specific skill set or a fancy certification. You are in the way because you are avoiding the internal work that actually moves the needle.

The Leverage Point: Happiness isn't something you earn later. It's the fuel you need *now* to get where you're going.

Stop waiting for the world to give you permission to be whole. Go back to the aisle. Make a different choice.

Now, get out of your own way.

Chapter 4

Information is Power (But Only if it's Clear)

If you asked ten of your employees to describe what your company stands for, would you get one clear answer or ten different ones? If you're like most leaders, the variety in their responses would be terrifying.

A company without a clear, unified message is like a ship without a rudder. Different departments drift in different directions, employees get confused about priorities, and customers don't understand why they should choose you. Information is power, but disorganized, inconsistent information creates chaos.

This chapter is about forging that clarity. We'll walk through the process of defining your core message, aligning your internal team behind it, and then broadcasting it to the world with confidence and consistency.

Step 1: The Source — Define Your Core Message

Before you can communicate anything, you have to know what you stand for. This isn't about fluffy marketing slogans; it's about digging down to the unshakable foundation of your business. This foundation has three parts:

- **Your Values:** *How You Behave.* These are the non-negotiable principles that guide every decision. They are the answer to the question, "How do we do things around here?" Are you driven by innovation, reliability, or community spirit? Define 3-5 core values that are authentic to you. A key question to ask yourself is: Do my personal values align with these, and do I maintain the professional boundaries to lead with them effectively?
- **Your Mission:** *Why You Exist.* This is your purpose, stated clearly and simply. It's the problem you solve for your customers. A mission isn't "to be profitable"; that's a result. A mission is "to make sustainable packaging accessible to small businesses" or "to provide reliable IT support for non-profits." What is your fundamental contribution?
- **Your Vision:** *Where You Are Going.* This is your long-term aspiration. It's the inspiring, ambitious future you are working to create. Your vision should feel a little bit scary and exciting. It's the destination on your map that energizes the entire crew for the long journey ahead.

Once you have a draft of these, gather your leadership team. Brainstorm key phrases and concepts on a whiteboard. Create a word cloud from the results to see which themes resonate most strongly. Practice saying your mission out loud until it feels natural and powerful. This core message is the source from which all communication will flow.

Step 2: Internal Alignment — Get Your Team on the Same Page

Your employees are your most important audience. If they don't understand or believe in your message, your customers never will. Your goal is to turn every employee into a confident ambassador for your brand.

- **Lead by Example:** Your values mean nothing if you don't live them. If you value transparency, you must be transparent. If you value teamwork, you must be collaborative. Your team will mirror your actions, not your words.
- **Integrate and Reinforce:** Weave your message into the fabric of the company. Discuss it during onboarding. Reference it in performance reviews. Celebrate team members who exemplify your values.
- **Use a Consistent Communication Rhythm:** Don’t let your message fade after a single announcement. Keep it alive with a steady drumbeat of internal communication. But remember, a meeting without a clear objective is a waste of everyone's time.

Your Internal Toolkit:

- **Regular Team Huddles:** Weekly meetings to discuss progress and challenges, always framed within the context of your mission.
- **Company-Wide "State of the Union":** Monthly or quarterly updates sharing news, celebrating wins, and reinforcing the vision.
- **Collaboration Hubs (Slack/Teams):** For real-time project collaboration and informal reinforcement of your culture.

- **Feedback Channels:** Anonymous surveys or suggestion boxes to show you value your team's insights and are living up to your own standards.

Step 3: External Resonance — Broadcast a Clear, Consistent Signal

Once your internal house is in order, you can project your message outward with power and consistency. Every piece of external communication should be a reflection of your core values and mission.

- **One Voice, Many Channels:** Whether it's a press release, a social media post, a sales brochure, or a customer support chat, the tone and message should feel consistent. This builds brand recognition and trust.
- **Engage, Don't Just Announce:** Communication is a two-way street. Use your external channels to listen as much as you talk. Engage with stakeholders—your customers, investors, and suppliers—by asking for their feedback and showing them how their input shapes your direction.
- **Be Strategic with Stakeholders:** Recognize that different stakeholders need different information.
    - **Customers** need to know how you solve their problems.
    - **Investors** need to see your financial health and long-term vision.
    - **Suppliers** need to understand your needs and opportunities for partnership. Tailor your engagement, but ensure the core message remains consistent for all.

Your External Toolkit:

- **Press Releases & Media Outreach:** For major announcements and building credibility.
- **Social Media:** To engage with your community, share your culture, and listen to your customers.

- **Email Marketing:** To keep your audience informed about products, services, and insights that reflect your brand's expertise.
- **Webinars & Events:** To educate your market and build direct relationships.
- **Customer Support:** As a frontline opportunity to live your values and gather crucial feedback.

Great companies are master communicators. Nike's "Just Do It" is a powerful distillation of their mission to inspire athletes. Starbucks' commitment "to inspire and nurture the human spirit" informs everything from their store design to their customer service. Their messages are clear, consistent, and authentic.

Your message, like your business, must also be ready to adapt. As markets shift, you may need to refine *how* you communicate your values, but the core itself should remain your guiding star.

Chapter Takeaway

Clarity is a force multiplier. When you distill your company's purpose into a clear, powerful message and ensure that the message is understood and lived by everyone internally, your external communications become exponentially more effective. A unified message aligns your team, builds trust with your customers, and provides a stable rudder in a chaotic sea.

Try This: Your One-Page "Clarity Charter"

In a notebook or a new document, draft the "source of truth" for your company's identity by answering these three core questions.

1. **Our Values: How do we behave?**
    - List the 3-5 non-negotiable principles that guide your company's actions. (Think in verbs and actions, not generic fluff).
2. **Our Mission: Why do we exist?**
    - In one single, jargon-free sentence, describe the problem you solve and for whom.
3. **Our Vision: Where are we going?**
    - Describe the inspiring future you are trying to create. Where will your company be in 3-5 years if you succeed?

Chapter 5

Beyond the PowerPoint: Making Your Message Real

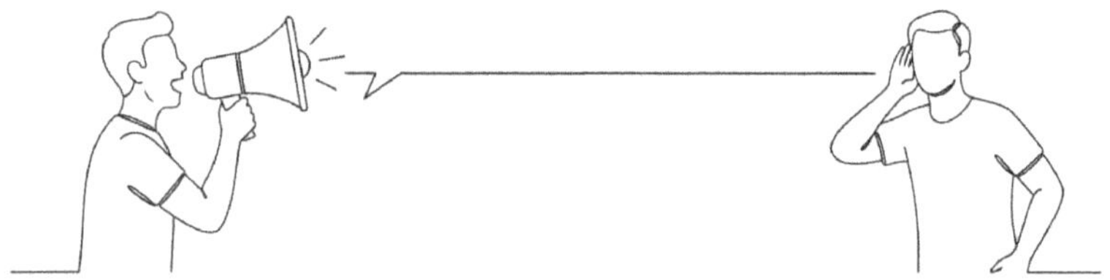

You've done the hard work. You've wrestled with ideas and defined your company's core message—its values, mission, and vision. You've captured it perfectly on a PowerPoint slide.

Now what?

A brilliant message that lives only in a presentation or on a poster is useless. It's shelfware. The real work begins now: embedding that message so deeply into your company culture that it becomes the default way of thinking, acting, and making decisions. This is how you move your message from a simple **broadcast** to a deeply held **belief**.

Part 1: The Broadcast — Make the Message Unavoidable

Your first job is to ensure that no employee can plausibly say, "I've never heard that before." You need to create a "surround sound" effect where your core message is communicated clearly, consistently, and through multiple channels.

- **Use Every Channel:** People absorb information differently. Some read every email; others only pay attention in meetings. Use a mix of channels to maximize reach: company-wide town halls, weekly team huddles, email newsletters, your intranet, and collaboration platforms like Slack or Teams.
- **Keep it Consistent:** The message must be the same everywhere. If your town hall speech is about innovation but your internal emails only talk about cutting costs, you're creating confusion, not clarity.
- **Frame it with a Story:** Don't just state the message; wrap it in a compelling narrative. Share stories of how a company value led to a customer success, or how a team's actions embodied the mission. Stories create an emotional connection that bullet points never will.

Part 2: The Integration — Weave the Message into the Daily Fabric

Once people have heard the message, you need to make it part of their daily work. It has to show up in the systems and processes they use every day.

- **Train for It:** Don't assume people know *how* to act on the message. If a core value is "Extreme Ownership," provide training on what that looks like in practice. Give them the tools and frameworks to succeed.

- **Put it in the Job Description:** Embed your values into your hiring and performance review processes. Ask interview questions related to your core message. Evaluate employees not just on *what* they achieve, but *how* they achieve it in relation to your company's values.
- **Make it Visual:** The physical (and digital) environment should constantly reinforce the message. Use posters, digital screens, and even team swag as regular, subtle reminders of what you stand for.

Part 3: The Reinforcement — From Understanding to Belief

This is the most important step. It's where you use human connection and recognition to turn intellectual understanding into genuine emotional buy-in.

- **Leaders Go First:** Your actions speak louder than any poster. You must be the most visible and consistent model of the message. If you want a culture of feedback, you must actively seek it out and receive it gracefully. If you want a culture of teamwork, you must celebrate collaboration and share credit. Your team is watching, and they will follow your lead.
- **What Gets Celebrated Gets Repeated:** Create a system to recognize and reward employees who live the message. This doesn't have to be a big bonus. A public shout-out in a company meeting or a heartfelt thank-you note can be incredibly powerful. When you throw a spotlight on desired behaviors, you're showing everyone else what success looks like in your culture.
- **Empower Employee Champions:** Involve your team in the process. Create committees or task forces dedicated to bringing specific values to life. When employees have a hand in shaping how the message is implemented, they take ownership of it. They move from being the audience to being co-authors.

Part 4: The Feedback Loop — Keep the Message Alive

Embedding a message isn't a one-time project; it's an ongoing process. You need to constantly measure whether your message is landing effectively and be ready to adapt.

- **Measure What Matters:** Establish Key Performance Indicators (KPIs) to track the message's impact. If your goal is to improve collaboration, track metrics from project management tools or ask about it in surveys.
- **Ask and Listen:** Use employee surveys, focus groups, and informal check-ins to gather direct feedback. Ask questions like, "On a scale of 1-10, how well do you feel we are living our value of 'Customer Obsession'?" or "Which communication channel do you find most useful for company updates?"
- **Adapt Your Strategy:** Use the data you collect. If email open rates are plummeting, it's a sign that your content isn't resonating. If employees love video messages from the CEO, do more of them. Be flexible and responsive to what works.

This cycle of broadcasting, integrating, reinforcing, and listening is what keeps a company culture alive, healthy, and aligned with its core purpose.

Chapter Takeaway

A message becomes culture when it’s no longer just a message—it's the way things are done. This transformation requires a relentless, multi-faceted effort from leadership. By clearly and consistently communicating your message, weaving it into your daily operations, celebrating those who live it, and listening to your team, you can build an influential culture that drives alignment, boosts performance, and helps you stand out as a leader in your industry.

Try This: The Message-Culture Consistency Check

To see where your message truly comes alive versus just being words on a wall, grab a notebook and run this simple audit.

First, pick one of your core company values. (e.g., "We Default to Transparency").

Next, rate how well that value shows up in these four key areas on a scale of 1 (Not at all) to 5 (This is a huge strength).

1. **Leadership Behavior:** Are my leaders and I consistently modeling this value?
2. **Daily Operations:** Is this value built into our core processes?
3. **Recognition & Rewards:** Do we publicly celebrate people who demonstrate this value?
4. **Hiring & Onboarding:** Do we screen for this value and teach it to new hires?
   truly comes alive versus just being
   an influential

Add up your scores. The areas with the lowest numbers are your starting point for improvement.

Chapter 6

Hiring Rockstars & Firing Roadblocks

A leader without a great team is like a world-class race car driver sitting in a rusty pickup truck. You can have all the skill, vision, and determination in the world, but you're not going to win any championships.

Of all the tasks that land on your desk, none are more critical than the decisions you make about people. Every person you bring onto your team either adds horsepower to your engine or creates drag. Your most important job—more important than strategy, more important than finance, more important than marketing—is to be the fierce, relentless gatekeeper of your team's talent.

This means mastering the two most difficult and impactful leadership skills: hiring the absolute best, and having the courage to remove those who are holding the team back.

Hiring the Rockstars

We've all heard the old mantra: "Hire slow, fire fast." It sounds wise, but it's often terrible advice. "Hire slow" can mean losing a brilliant candidate to a faster competitor, and "fire fast" can be reckless and cruel.

Let's use a better mantra: **Hire Deliberately, Fire Decisively.**

Hiring deliberately means you don't just fill a seat; you find the right person for your specific culture and goals. This requires you to look beyond the resume. A resume tells you what someone has *done*, but it tells you nothing about *who they are*. Hiring based on a resume alone is like marrying someone based on their dating profile; the real person is probably different, and they might not actually enjoy "long walks on the beach" with your company's budget.

To hire deliberately, you need to interview for attitude and aptitude, not just past accomplishments.

- **Go Beyond "What" and Ask "How":** Don't just ask, "Did you increase sales at your last job?" Ask, "Tell me *how* you increased sales. What was your specific strategy? What obstacles did you hit? Who did you need to collaborate with to make it happen?" This uncovers their thought process, their resilience, and whether they are a "we" or a "me" player.
- **Use the "Teach Me Something" Test:** Ask the candidate to take five minutes to teach you something they are passionate about, whether it's a complex work topic or the basics of beekeeping. This simple test reveals more than a dozen standard interview questions. It shows you their ability to communicate complex

ideas clearly and, more importantly, it reveals their level of passion and energy.
- **Conduct Reference Checks That Matter:** Don't just call the references they give you; that list is curated to perfection. Instead, ask their reference this magic question: "Who else worked closely with them on that project that you think I should talk to?" This gets you "off the record" and closer to the unvarnished truth.

Firing the Roadblocks

This is the part of the job nobody likes. But your refusal to make a tough call is a bigger act of cruelty to your team than the firing itself. There are two kinds of roadblocks you must remove: the **Nice-But-Ineffective B-Player** and the **High-Performing-But-Toxic A-Player**.

The B-Player is the person who is wonderful to be around but consistently fails to deliver the results you need. The Toxic A-Player is the person who hits all their numbers but leaves a trail of bruised and demoralized colleagues in their wake.

Keeping either on your team is a cancer. It tells your true rockstars that you either tolerate mediocrity or you condone toxicity. They will be the first to leave, tired of cleaning up messes or enduring abuse. Keeping a toxic employee because they're "good at their job" is like keeping a pet scorpion because it's "good at catching flies." Sure, but the constant threat of being stung will eventually become a problem for everyone.

I learned this lesson in one of the most difficult situations of my career. I had a designer on my team who was brilliant—truly one of the most talented creatives I'd ever worked with. We also had a great personal relationship, and I considered him a friend.

But he started going through some incredibly difficult personal challenges, and his work began to suffer. Deadlines were missed. Details were overlooked. The quality that had once been his signature was gone. I found myself stepping in to fix things, first occasionally, and then constantly. I was essentially doing two jobs: my own, and the most critical parts of his. My support for him was inadvertently enabling his lack of performance and creating a massive bottleneck for the entire team.

We talked through his challenges together, multiple times. I was empathetic to his struggles, but I also had to be direct about the impact on the business. We went through the process of official warnings and performance discussions, but nothing changed.

Finally, I had to make the decision to let him go. It was awful. I was losing a friend and a person whose talent I deeply respected. Every part of me wanted to give him just one more chance. But I realized that keeping him wasn't an act of compassion; it was an act of conflict avoidance that was hurting him, the team, and the business.

The surprising thing happened *after* I let him go. Freed from the pressure of a job he could no longer perform, he got the push he needed to sort out his personal issues and rediscover his internal drive. A few months later, he called to tell me he'd found a new job that was a much better fit for him and to thank me. He's thriving now.

That experience taught me a crucial lesson: sometimes the most compassionate act a leader can perform is to make a clean, decisive break. It allows the person to find a place where they can truly succeed, and it allows your team to get back to full strength. It's a painful decision, but your responsibility is to the health of the entire team, not just the comfort of one individual.

Firing someone should never be a surprise. It should be the final, respectful step in a clear process.

1. **Give Clear, Direct Feedback:** The employee must know exactly where they are falling short. This feedback should be documented and specific.
2. **Create a Performance Improvement Plan (PIP):** Give them a clear, written plan with measurable goals and a specific timeline (e.g., 30 or 60 days) to improve. Offer your support and check in regularly. This gives them a genuine chance to succeed.
3. **Make the Decision:** If, after that period, the performance or behavior hasn't improved to the required level, your decision has been made for you. It's no longer personal; it's procedural.

When it's time for the final conversation, be decisive and humane.

- **Be Direct and Clear:** Get straight to the point. "I'm letting you go, and your last day will be today." Don't use vague language that gives false hope.
- **Keep It Short:** This is not a debate. The decision is final. Explain briefly that they were unable to meet the requirements of the PIP, and leave it at that.
- **Be Prepared:** Have all the necessary paperwork, severance information, and logistical details ready beforehand.
- **Be Human:** End the conversation with dignity. You can say something like, "I know this is difficult news, and I want to thank you for your efforts here. I wish you the best in finding a role that is a better fit for your talents."

Chapter Takeaway

Your company will never be more effective than the people on your team. As a leader, you are the chief talent officer and the guardian at the gate. Having the diligence to hire the right people and the courage to remove the wrong ones are not side tasks in your job—they *are* the job. Master these two skills, and you will have built a team capable of achieving anything.

Try This: The Rockstar Scorecard

The next time you interview a promising candidate, use this framework to evaluate them beyond their resume. In a notebook, score them from 1-10 in these three key areas.

1. The Skills Score: Based on their resume and technical interview, how confident are you that this person has the raw skills to do the job? **(Score: ___ / 10)**

2. The Attitude Score: Based on their answers to situational questions (like "Tell me about a time you failed"), how much do you want this person's attitude and way of working on your team? **(Score: ___ / 10)**

3. The Culture Fit Score: Based on how they talk about their values and past collaborations, how well does this person align with your company's non-negotiable values? **(Score: ___ / 10)**

A true "Rockstar" scores highly (8+) in all three categories. This method helps you see the whole picture and avoid hiring a "toxic A-player."

Chapter 7

Built for Speed: People, Structure, and Communication in an Agile World

In a traditional company, information and decisions flow like a waterfall: starting at the top, cascading down through layers of management, and finally reaching the people doing the work. It's orderly, predictable, and worked fine in a slower-moving world.

But what happens when the landscape changes overnight? The waterfall goes right over a cliff.

Today's market doesn't reward rigid, top-down structures. It rewards speed, adaptability, and resilience. It rewards organizations that are **Agile**.

Originating in software development, Agile is more than just a process; it's a mindset for thriving in an environment of constant change. It's about empowered teams, rapid feedback loops, and continuous improvement. This chapter is about taking Agile out of the tech department and applying its core principles to the very fabric of your business: your people, your structure, and how you all communicate.

Part 1: Agile People — From Cogs to Creative Engines

An Agile organization is built on a foundation of motivated, trusted individuals. It's a fundamental shift from viewing people as resources who execute tasks to seeing them as creative engines who solve problems.

- **Build Projects Around Motivated People:** Agile's success depends on giving talented people the environment and support they need, then getting out of their way. This means trusting your team to make decisions about their work without micromanaging them into oblivion.
- **Champion Cross-Functional Teams:** Silos are the enemy of speed. An Agile structure favors cross-functional teams where designers, developers, marketers, and salespeople work *together* on a single project. This demolishes the "us vs. them" mentality and ensures all perspectives are in the room from day one, leading to smarter, faster solutions.
- **Let the Best Ideas Emerge:** In a traditional hierarchy, ideas have to fight their way up the chain of command. In an Agile environment, the best architectures, requirements, and designs emerge from self-organizing teams—the people closest to the work. Your job as a leader is to foster the conditions for this to happen, not to be the sole source of brilliant ideas.

Part 2: Agile Structure — From a Pyramid to a Network

You can't have Agile people working in a rigid, bureaucratic structure. You have to reshape the organization itself to be as flexible and responsive as you need your teams to be.

- **Embrace Change as a Strategy:** A core tenet of Agile is welcoming changing requirements, even late in the game. A rigid structure is brittle; it shatters when hit with unexpected change. An Agile structure is designed to bend without breaking. It sees a shift in customer needs not as a crisis, but as an opportunity to deliver more value.
- **Simplify and Eliminate Redundancy:** Agile prizes simplicity—what it calls "the art of maximizing the amount of work *not* done." Take a hard look at your processes. Are two departments submitting similar reports? Do approvals have to go through five layers of management? Every redundant task and unnecessary layer of bureaucracy you eliminate is a burst of speed for your organization.
- **Focus on a Sustainable Pace:** An Agile structure isn't about burning people out with endless sprints. It's about creating a sustainable pace where technical excellence and good design can flourish. By eliminating waste and focusing on high-value work, teams can maintain momentum without sacrificing quality or well-being.

Part 3: Agile Communication — From Formal Reports to Fluid Conversation

Clear, rapid communication is the lifeblood of an Agile organization. The goal is to shrink the distance between a question being asked and an answer being given. This requires a modern communication strategy and the right technology to power it.

- **Prioritize High-Bandwidth Communication:** An Agile principle states that "face-to-face conversation is the most effective method of conveying information." In a hybrid or remote world, this translates to prioritizing video calls over long email chains for complex discussions. You can read body language and nuance, solve problems in minutes that would take days over email, and build real human connection.
- **Use Technology to Create Transparency:** The right tools are essential. They don't just enable communication; they create a transparent and aligned work environment.
    - **Instant Messaging (Slack, Teams):** Perfect for quick questions, real-time updates, and reducing email clutter. Create project-specific channels to keep conversations organized and accessible.
    - **Collaborative Software (Google Workspace, Microsoft 365):** These tools allow teams to work on documents and presentations simultaneously, turning review cycles from a slow, multi-day process into a real-time collaboration.
    - **Project Management Platforms (Asana, Trello, Monday.com):** These are crucial for making work visible. They outline objectives, assign tasks, and track progress openly, ensuring everyone knows the status of a project at a glance.
- **Establish a Communication Rhythm:** Create a predictable cadence of communication, such as daily stand-ups, weekly check-ins, and monthly reviews. This routine ensures that information flows consistently and that teams regularly reflect on how to become more effective—the cornerstone of continuous improvement.

Chapter Takeaway

Building an Agile organization is about fundamentally reshaping how your company operates. By applying Agile principles to your people (empowering them), your structure (making it flexible), and your communication (making it transparent and rapid), you create a business that can not only survive but thrive in a world of constant change. It's a shift from a rigid, slow-moving machine to a dynamic, adaptable organism.

Try This: Your 5-Minute Agile Audit

"Agile" can feel like a vague buzzword. To get a real sense of how adaptable your team or organization actually is, grab a notebook, a piece of paper, or open a new digital document for this quick audit.

The goal is to get an honest snapshot of your team's agility. For each of the following six statements, give yourself a score from 1 (Not at all) to 5 (This is our standard practice).

1. **Our People:**
    - My team members are empowered to make decisions about their own work without needing multiple layers of approval.
    - We have true cross-functional collaboration, where people from different departments (e.g., marketing, sales, product) work together on projects from the start.
2. **Our Structure:**
    - When a customer's needs or market conditions change, our team can pivot its priorities quickly without a crisis.
    - We actively seek to simplify our processes and eliminate redundant tasks or reports.

3. Our Communication:

- Information about key projects and goals is transparent and easily accessible to everyone on the team.
- We have a regular, consistent rhythm of check-ins (like daily stand-ups or weekly reviews) to discuss progress and roadblocks.

Calculate Your Score: Now, add up your six scores to get your **Total Agility Score** out of a possible 30.

A low score reveals that your organization is still operating with a rigid, "waterfall" mindset. The specific areas where you scored lowest are your starting points for building a faster, more adaptable, and truly Agile culture.

Chapter 8

The Meeting That Should Have Been an Email: A Guide to Productive Gatherings

Early in my corporate career, I was part of a mandatory weekly "synergy" meeting. On paper, it was crucial. It brought together multiple teams—IT, programming, and design—to align on our most important projects. In reality, it was a masterclass in what not to do.

Every week, the meeting would devolve into the same soul-crushing ritual, which I privately called the "Blame Carousel." A problem would be raised, and then the ride would begin. The IT team would blame the programming team for buggy code. The programming team would then blame the design team for creating unrealistic mockups. To complete the circle, the design team would blame IT for having slow servers. Round and round it went.

And at the center of this carousel was the leader, a man who seemed to run on a volatile mixture of pure rage and incompetence. Instead of facilitating solutions, he would lose his temper, publicly berate people, and encourage the finger-pointing. The air in the room was thick with fear. No one dared offer a real idea, and admitting a mistake was professional suicide.

We would all file out of that room an hour later feeling drained, resentful, and with absolutely no clear direction. Nothing was ever solved. No action items were ever assigned. It was a complete waste of our collective time and talent, all disguised as a "crucial" weekly meeting.

That experience taught me everything about how *not* to lead. It showed me that bad meetings are the silent thieves of productivity, draining morale and grinding progress to a halt. As a leader, your job is to declare war on them.

The Triage: Does This Meeting Even Need to Exist?

Before scheduling a meeting, you must act as a ruthless triage nurse. Your calendar is not a public park where anyone can have a picnic; it is a strategic asset. Most of the things we call "meetings" are just poorly disguised requests for information.

There are only **three legitimate reasons** to pull a group of people into a room together:

1. **To Make a Decision:** A specific, debatable choice must be made, and you need the key stakeholders to discuss the options and align on a final path forward. The goal is a concrete decision.
2. **To Brainstorm & Create:** A complex problem needs the friction of different minds rubbing together to generate new, creative

solutions. The goal is a whiteboard full of new ideas that didn't exist before the meeting.

3. **To Build Connection & Morale:** This includes one-on-ones, team-building events, or celebrating a major win. The primary goal is strengthening human relationships and team cohesion.

If your purpose does not fall into one of those three buckets, **it must be an email, a report, or a chat message.** A status update is an email. A request for data is a chat message. A company announcement is a memo. Defend your team's time as fiercely as you defend your budget.

The Golden Rule: No Agenda, No Attenda

This is the one law you must never break. A meeting invitation without an agenda is not a meeting; it's an ambush. It's a sign of disrespect for everyone's time.

Empower your entire team—including yourself—to politely decline any meeting invitation that doesn't have a clear agenda. This simple rule will single-handedly eliminate half of the useless meetings in your organization overnight.

A proper agenda is not just a list of topics. It must answer three questions:

- **Why are we here?** A single sentence stating the desired outcome. (e.g., *"By the end of this meeting, we will decide on the final design for the Q4 ad campaign."*)
- **What are we discussing?** A short, bulleted list of the specific questions or topics that will lead to the outcome.
- **Who needs to be here (and why)?** A list of attendees and their roles. If you can't justify someone's presence, don't invite them. It's a sign of respect to *not* invite someone to a meeting they don't need to be in.

The Art of Facilitation: How to Run the Room

Your job as the meeting leader is not to be the star of the show; it is to be the facilitator who guides the conversation to a productive conclusion.

- **Start on Time. End on Time. Period.** Better yet, end five minutes early. This is the single easiest way to earn the respect and gratitude of your team.
- **Assign Roles:** At the start of the meeting, designate a **Note-Taker** (responsible for capturing action items) and a **Timekeeper** (responsible for politely saying, "We have ten minutes left for this topic"). This can be as simple as using AI for video calls or recording the meeting and then using AI afterward to create a summary and a list of actions.
- **Be the Polite Sheepdog:** Your main job is to herd the conversation. When it starts to stray into unrelated topics, it's your responsibility to gently but firmly guide it back. "That's an interesting point, Bob, but let's table that for now and make sure we resolve our main agenda item."
- **Mine for Conflict:** A good meeting isn't always harmonious. Healthy debate is how you get to the best decisions. Actively solicit opinions from quieter team members. "Sarah, we haven't heard from you on this. Do you see any risks we're missing?"

The Follow-Up: Making Sure the Meeting Mattered

A meeting without a follow-up is a conversation that evaporates into thin air, leaving no trace of accountability. The work isn't over when the meeting ends.

Within an hour of the meeting, the designated note-taker must send out a brief summary. It shouldn't be a long transcript. It should contain only one thing: a simple table with three columns.

The Action Item (What needs to be done?)	Who Owns It?	By When?
Finalize the budget spreadsheet.	Jane	Friday, 5 PM
Send the revised proposal to the client.	David	EOD Today
Schedule the follow-up brainstorming session.	Michael	Tomorrow

This simple format creates instant clarity, assigns ownership, and establishes deadlines. It is the bridge between conversation and action.

Chapter Takeaway

Meetings are not inherently evil. *Poorly run* meetings are. They are a symptom of lazy thinking and a disrespect for people's time. By treating meetings as a high-cost activity—to be used deliberately, planned carefully, and executed with discipline—you can transform your organization's most-hated ritual into its most powerful tool for making smart decisions and driving results.

Chapter 9

The War on Waste: How to Fix Your Processes and Stop Bleeding Money

Every business has a hidden tax that bleeds it dry, day after day. It's not a government tax; it's the "Waste Tax"—a silent killer composed of clunky processes, redundant tasks, squandered resources, and outdated thinking.

This tax doesn't show up as a line item on your P&L, but you pay for it constantly in the form of frustrated employees, missed deadlines, and bloated expenses. Your job as a leader is to become a waste detective—to hunt down inefficiency in all its forms and declare a company-wide war on it.

This war is fought on two main fronts: the battle against **wasted time** (your processes) and the battle against **wasted money** (your resources). Winning on both fronts is essential for building a lean, agile, and profitable organization.

Battleground 1: Wasted Time — Fixing Your Processes

Inefficient processes are the breeding ground for wasted time. They are the endless approval chains, the duplicated data entry, and the pointless meetings that drain your team's energy and focus. Here's how you fight back.

- **Map the Battlefield:** You can't fix a process you don't understand. Start by mapping out your key workflows from beginning to end. Create a visual chart of every single step. When you force yourself to document the process, the absurdities often jump right off the page. "Wait, this has to be approved by *four* different people?" or "Why are we entering the same information into three different systems?"
- **Empower Your Frontline Soldiers:** The people doing the work every day know the processes better than anyone. They know what's clunky and what's slow. Create channels—regular meetings, surveys, suggestion boxes—for them to provide feedback without fear of reprisal. When a customer service rep tells you a specific software tool is slowing them down, listen. Their insight is gold.
- **Measure Everything:** Use performance metrics as your reconnaissance. Track how long it takes to complete key tasks. If a certain process consistently takes longer than expected, that's a red flag telling you where to focus your attention. Clear metrics allow you to move from guessing to knowing.
- **Automate the Grunt Work:** In today's world, no human should be doing repetitive, manual data entry. Use automation tools to

handle these tasks. This not only saves enormous amounts of time and reduces errors but also frees up your employees to focus on strategic, high-value activities that actually require a human brain.

Battleground 2: Wasted Money — Optimizing Your Resources

Wasted time is only half the battle. The other, more insidious enemy is wasted money—the silent drain on your resources from outdated technology, poor vendor management, and inefficient resource allocation.

Through my company, I've worked extensively with builders and construction companies. It's an industry where waste can be obvious—if you know where to look. I was working with one home builder whose job sites were a graveyard of lost profits. At the end of every build, there were piles of unused lumber, boxes of extra tiles, and stacks of drywall offcuts—all paid for, all destined for the dumpster.

The problem wasn't bad craftsmanship; it was terrible planning. Their ordering process was based on guesswork and a "better safe than sorry" mentality. They were so afraid of running out of materials and delaying a project that they habitually over-ordered everything. This created a massive, hidden "waste tax" on every single home they built.

We sat down and reviewed their entire ordering and inventory process from start to finish. We examined the blueprints, analyzed the actual material usage from past projects, and compared it to their purchasing patterns. By establishing new, data-driven norms for quantity and quality—" for this model home, we need exactly X linear feet of baseboard, not X plus 20% 'just in case' "—we transformed their system.

The result was immediate. The dumpsters were less full, material costs on every project dropped, and their bottom line grew significantly. It was a perfect example of how fighting waste isn't about being cheap; it's about being smart.

- **Upgrade Your Arsenal (Technology):** Clinging to outdated, on-premise technology is a classic case of being "penny-wise and pound-foolish."
    - **Cloud Computing:** Moving from physical servers to the cloud can slash hardware, maintenance, and energy costs by up to 50%. It also makes your tech team faster and more innovative.
    - **Automation & AI:** Automating tasks like invoice processing or basic customer support can save hundreds of thousands in labor costs while freeing up your team for more complex issues.
    - **Unified Communications:** For remote or international teams, robust virtual meeting platforms can erase tens of thousands in travel costs annually while streamlining collaboration.
- **Conduct a Resource Audit:** Scrutinize where your money is going.
    - **Energy:** An energy audit and a switch to efficient lighting and climate control can cut utility bills by 10-30%.
    - **Inventory:** Are you paying to store excess products that might spoil or become obsolete? Better demand forecasting can cut these costs by 20% or more.
    - **Software Subscriptions:** Do a "subscription audit." You will almost certainly find overlapping or "zombie" licenses for software nobody uses, potentially saving you tens of thousands a year.
- **Spend Smarter, Not Less:**
    - **Outsource Non-Core Functions:** Do you really need a full-time in-house team for payroll or basic IT support?

    Outsourcing specialized tasks to external providers is often cheaper and more effective, freeing your team to focus on what they do best.
    - **Renegotiate Everything:** Regularly review your vendor contracts. Don't just auto-renew. Market conditions change, and a simple renegotiation could yield a 10-15% price cut on raw materials or services.

Building Your Army: Create a Culture of Continuous Improvement

You cannot win the war on waste alone. You need to enlist every single employee as a waste detective. This requires a cultural shift.

- **Train and Develop:** Invest in your team's skills. Well-trained employees make fewer errors, work more efficiently, and are better equipped to identify and solve problems. An upfront investment of $20,000 in training can easily prevent a $50,000 quality issue down the line.
- **Reward Efficiency:** Create feedback loops where employees are encouraged and rewarded for finding and eliminating waste. When a frontline employee's idea saves the company thousands of hours, celebrate them publicly. What gets rewarded gets repeated.
- **Use Balanced Metrics:** As you track cost savings, make sure you're also tracking customer satisfaction and employee engagement. This ensures your cost-cutting efforts don't come at the expense of quality or morale.

Chapter Takeaway

Eliminating waste is one of the most powerful levers you can pull to improve your business. By systematically hunting down and eradicating wasted time in your processes and wasted money in your resource allocation, you do more than just improve your bottom line. You create a leaner, faster, and more resilient organization. Every dollar and hour you save is capital that can be reinvested into what really matters: innovation, growth, and future-proofing your company for the challenges ahead.

Chapter 10

The Data Storyteller: Turning Noise into Narrative

Your team just spent a month gathering data. They deliver a 50-page spreadsheet full of numbers, charts, and tables. It's thorough, it's accurate, and it's completely overwhelming.

What do you do? If you forward that spreadsheet to your boss or another department with a note that says "FYI," you've failed.

Data doesn't speak for itself. It has no voice. It's your job as a leader to give it one. You are the translator, the sense-maker, the storyteller. You have to dig into that mountain of information, find the single, crucial narrative hidden within it, and present that story so clearly and compellingly that it drives action. This chapter is about how to become your organization's essential Data Storyteller.

The Storyteller's Mindset: Find the "So What?"

Before you create a single chart, your first job is to answer the most important question: **"So what?"** What does this data *mean*? What is the single most important insight my audience needs to understand, and what do I want them to *do* about it?

Never start with the data and ask what it says. Start with the problem you're trying to solve and ask what data you need to tell the story. This mindset shifts you from being a passive presenter of facts to an active driver of decisions.

Choosing Your Language: The Visual Toolkit

Once you know the story you want to tell, you need to choose the right language to tell it. In data storytelling, your language is visual.

The Grammar of Graphics: Picking the Right Chart

Using the wrong chart is like using the wrong word; it confuses the message. Each chart type has a specific job.

- **Bar Charts:** Use these to **compare** distinct quantities. (e.g., Sales by region, website traffic by marketing channel). They are simple, clear, and instantly show "which of these is biggest?"
- **Line Charts:** Use these to show a **trend over time**. (e.g., Monthly revenue over the last year, stock price changes). They are the best way to answer, "How has this changed?"
- **Pie Charts:** Use these to show **parts of a single whole**. Use them sparingly and only for a few categories. (e.g., Market share breakdown between 3-4 competitors). If you have more than five slices, use a bar chart instead.

- **Scatter Plots:** Use these to show the **relationship between two different variables**. They help answer, "Does X affect Y?" (e.g., Does advertising spend correlate with sales revenue?).
- **Heat Maps:** Use these to show **intensity or concentration**. (e.g., Visualizing which parts of your website get the most clicks, or sales performance across different states).
- **Gantt Charts & Kanban Boards:** These aren't for numerical data, but for telling a story about **process and workflow**. A Gantt chart tells a story about a project's timeline, while a Kanban board tells a story about a team's current workload and progress.

The Storyteller's Tools: From Slides to Visuals

You have more tools at your disposal than ever before to bring your data stories to life.

The Classics (PowerPoint & Keynote): These are the industry standards for a reason. They are powerful, versatile, and everyone knows how to use them. They are perfect for creating the charts listed above and building a traditional, linear presentation. Don't underestimate their power when used well.

The AI-Powered Innovator (Gamma): For those who want to create stunning presentations, documents, or web pages without the design headache, Gamma is a game-changer.

> **Gamma.app**
> Create stunning presentations, docs, and web pages—AI-fast and beautifully simple.
>
> Gamma is an AI-powered platform that instantly transforms your text-based ideas into polished, professional, and web-friendly presentations. Instead of fussing with slide masters and text boxes, you focus on the content, and Gamma handles the

design. It's ideal for creating interactive, mobile-friendly decks, reports, and sales collateral that feel more modern than a traditional slideshow. Its real-time collaboration features also make it perfect for teams.

The Infographic Specialists (Canva, Piktochart, Visme): When you need to combine multiple charts, icons, and text into a single, shareable image, these tools are your best friend. They are template-driven and user-friendly, allowing you to create beautiful infographics that tell a complex story at a glance. They are perfect for social media, newsletters, and internal reports.

Advanced Language: Audio & Video

To make your story truly resonate, engage more senses.

- **Audio:** A simple voice-over on a slide can explain the nuances of a complex chart, guiding your audience's attention just as you would if you were in the room with them.
- **Video:** A short video can bring data to life. Imagine showing a chart of declining customer satisfaction, immediately followed by a 30-second video clip of a customer testimonial explaining their frustration. This creates an emotional connection to the data that numbers alone never could.

Telling a Great Data Story: Best Practices

Knowing the language and having the tools is only half the battle. Great storytellers follow a few simple rules.

- **One Slide, One Idea:** Each slide or visual should have a single, clear purpose. Don't cram five different charts onto one slide. Give your key insights room to breathe.
- **Declutter Aggressively:** Remove everything that doesn't support your story—unnecessary gridlines, redundant labels, 3D

effects, background noise. The simpler the visual, the more powerful its message.

- **Use Color with Purpose:** Don't use color for decoration. Use it strategically to highlight your main point. Make most of your chart a neutral color (like gray) and use a single, bright color to draw the eye to the most important data point.
- **Tell Your Audience What to Think:** Don't just label your chart "Quarterly Sales." Give it a title that tells the story, like, "Q3 Sales Grew by 15%, Driven by the New Product Launch." Guide them to the conclusion you want them to reach.

Chapter Takeaway

Data is just raw material. It's the story you build with it that drives change. As a leader, your ability to transform a spreadsheet into a clear, compelling narrative is a superpower. By adopting a storyteller's mindset, choosing the right visual language, and following the rules of clear communication, you can ensure your insights are not just seen but understood, remembered, and acted upon.

Chapter 11

The Revenue Engine: Uniting Sales and Marketing for Explosive Growth

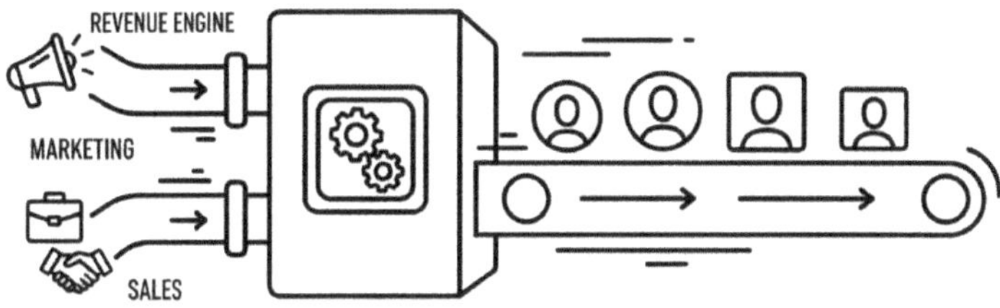

In most companies, the sales and marketing departments are like warring siblings forced to share a car. They both want to drive growth, but they're constantly fighting over the keys, the map, and who controls the radio. Marketing complains that Sales never follows up on their leads. Sales complains that Marketing's leads are garbage.

The result? A clunky, sputtering revenue engine that wastes time, burns cash, and leaves customers confused. Your job as a leader is to end this civil war. It's time to get your teams to stop working in silos and start building a single, high-performance revenue engine.

Part 1: Defining the Jobs — The Two Key Parts of the Engine

To get them working together, you first have to clarify their distinct roles. Think of it like a party:

- **Marketing is the promoter.** Their job is to create the buzz. They design the invitations, pick the theme, and make sure everyone knows that this is the party they can't miss. They are responsible for awareness and interest—the top of the funnel.
- **Sales is the host.** Their job is to work the room. They greet guests at the door, engage in personal conversations, answer questions, and make sure everyone has what they need to have a great time and commit to staying. They are responsible for conversion and closing deals—the bottom of the funnel.

Marketing's success is measured by the number of *qualified* people they bring to the party. Sales' success is measured by how many of those people they convert into committed fans. They have different jobs, but the same ultimate goal: a successful party (a thriving business).

Part 2: The Alignment Problem — Why Most Revenue Engines Sputter

The friction between sales and marketing usually comes from a few common, costly misconceptions. However, the most significant source of misalignment often originates from the top.

I learned this firsthand when I was hired as a part-time marketing director for an IT company. They had a substantial, experienced sales team and wanted to build a real marketing function to generate qualified leads for them. On paper, it was the perfect setup to build a powerful revenue engine.

But from day one, there was a fundamental disconnect. The owner, who had personally hired me to lead marketing, immediately started trying to pigeonhole me into a sales role. He wanted me to make calls and chase deals directly, rather than building the lead-generation system we had agreed upon.

The result was predictable chaos. The marketing engine we were supposed to build never even got off the ground. The sales team was completely confused—was I a colleague they should collaborate with, or a competitor chasing the same commissions? They didn't know what my role was. Frankly, neither did the owner who was signing my checks.

We had numerous meetings. I presented strategies, clarified the distinct roles of marketing (attracting and nurturing potential customers) and sales (converting those prospects into clients), and tried to align my efforts with the goals he had agreed to before I came on board. But I eventually realized the roadblock wasn't the team; it was the leader. He fundamentally saw marketing as just "another form of sales" and was never going to truly invest in it or empower it to function as a separate, strategic discipline.

Ultimately, I had to gracefully exit. You cannot fix an engine when the chief mechanic is determined to put the wrong parts in the wrong places. That experience was a powerful lesson: sales and marketing alignment isn't something the teams can figure out on their own. It has to be defined, championed, and protected by leadership. If the leader doesn't understand the difference, the engine will never run smoothly.

This kind of leadership confusion is often rooted in a few common myths.

- **The "More is Better" Myth:** Marketing generates 1,000 leads. They declare victory. But if 950 of those leads are unqualified, they've just overwhelmed the sales team with dead ends. The goal isn't more leads; it's more *qualified* leads.
- **The "Awareness is Enough" Trap:** A marketing campaign that gets a lot of buzz but doesn't lead to sales isn't a success; it's an expensive hobby. Brand awareness is important, but it must be paired with a clear strategy to convert that interest into revenue.
- **The "Technology Will Fix It" Fallacy:** Automation platforms and AI are powerful, but they are amplifiers, not saviors. They complement and supercharge a smart strategy; they cannot replace the human effort needed to understand customers and build real relationships.

When these misconceptions take hold, you get fragmented messaging, duplicated efforts, and a massive amount of wasted resources.

Part 3: The Solution — Building a Modern Revenue Engine

Building a high-performance engine requires two things: human alignment and a technology supercharger.

First, The Human Alignment Before any tool can help, your teams must be aligned. This is non-negotiable.

- **Mandate Communication:** Schedule regular, mandatory meetings between sales and marketing leaders. They must share insights, customer feedback, and data. Marketing needs to hear what customers are saying on sales calls, and sales needs to know what campaigns marketing is running.

- **Create Shared Goals:** Stop measuring the teams on separate metrics. Tie both marketing and sales performance to the same ultimate goal: **revenue growth.** When they share the same target, they are forced to work together to hit it.
- **Build a Unified Funnel:** Map out the *entire* customer journey, from the first marketing touchpoint to the final sales call. Define exactly when a lead is "marketing qualified" and when it becomes "sales qualified." This single source of truth eliminates the "your leads are bad" argument forever.

Second, The Technology Supercharger Once your teams are aligned, you pour high-octane fuel into the engine with the right technology. Not too long ago, I thought AI was mainly hype—something for tech geeks or billion-dollar companies. However, after experimenting with many tools, I quickly realized that this stuff works. Well, some of it!

I've been testing AI for sales and marketing, and it's been a total game-changer. It helps me move faster, get more done, and create better results—without burning out or overcomplicating everything.

Think: faster content, better leads, stronger outreach, and smoother workflows. And the best part? Most of these tools are plug-and-play. They don't require a high degree of technical knowledge.

Essential AI Tools you Should be Using

Hostinger

Launch and scale your online presence—fast, affordable, and AI-powered.

What it is:
Hostinger is an all-in-one web hosting platform designed for

startups, freelancers, and growing businesses that need fast, reliable, and scalable hosting. With built-in AI tools and a user-friendly website builder, Hostinger empowers anyone to create a mobile-optimized, professional-looking site in minutes—no coding required.

Why it's powerful for businesses:

- **AI Website Builder:** Quickly generate a complete, mobile-friendly website by answering a few simple questions—perfect for entrepreneurs who need to move fast.
- **Blazing-fast performance:** Hostinger's LiteSpeed servers and global CDN ensure your website loads quickly, which boosts SEO and keeps customers engaged.
- **All-in-one stack:** Includes domain registration, SSL, business email, WordPress hosting, and eCommerce tools in one affordable plan.
- **24/7 support:** Dedicated support team available around the clock to assist with any technical issues, migrations, or scaling questions.
- **Developer tools & integrations:** For those who need more customization, Hostinger supports Git, PHP, MySQL, and custom integrations.

Best use cases for businesses:

- **Quickly launch service pages** or landing pages for marketing campaigns
- **Create a sales-ready eCommerce site** without paying for a dev team
- **Host a high-performance blog** that drives organic traffic and captures leads
- **Offer client hosting services** as an agency with their reseller-friendly plans

---

Descript

Studio-quality video and podcast editing—without the studio.

What it is:
Descript is an all-in-one audio and video editing tool that lets you edit media content as easily as a Word doc. With powerful AI-driven features like transcription, voice cloning, and screen recording, it's built for business owners who want to produce professional content quickly and affordably.

Why it's powerful for businesses:

- **Edit by text:** Delete filler words, change narration, or move video segments just by editing the transcript.
- **Overdub:** Need a voiceover tweak? Just type the changes, and Descript's AI voice cloning will match your voice and tone seamlessly.
- **Screen recorder + video editor:** Ideal for demos, webinars, tutorials, and internal training content.
- **Polish fast:** Add subtitles, branding, music, and effects without hiring an editor.
- **Collaborative:** Great for teams producing recurring content like podcasts or YouTube series.

Best use cases for businesses:

- **Build authority** with podcasts, video newsletters, and expert interviews
- **Train teams or onboard clients** with polished internal how-to videos
- **Repurpose webinars or meetings** into short clips for social and email campaigns
- **Launch YouTube channels** without needing technical production skills

---

Writesonic

AI content + SEO strategy = faster growth.

What it is:
Writesonic is more than just a copywriting tool—it's a full-fledged AI-powered content engine that also helps businesses build and execute smart SEO strategies.

Why it's powerful for businesses:

- **Content at scale:** Create blog posts, landing pages, ads, and product descriptions in minutes. Writesonic's AI adapts to your brand voice, ensuring consistency across all channels.
- **SEO research built-in:** With features like keyword suggestions, SERP analysis, and content scoring, Writesonic helps you identify what to write *and* how to outrank competitors.
- **Article optimization:** It offers SEO tools that structure your content around top-ranking competitors, helping you optimize for Google's algorithm from the ground up.
- **AI article writer 5.0:** The latest update enables you to produce full-length, SEO-optimized articles based on minimal input—perfect for blogs, thought leadership, or long-form content marketing.
- **Integrations with Surfer SEO and Zapier:** Streamline your workflow by connecting Writesonic with other tools in your tech stack.

Best use cases for businesses:

- **Scale organic traffic** with consistent, optimized blog content
- **Launch landing pages** for PPC campaigns quickly
- **Test ad copy** variations to improve conversion rates
- **Repurpose content** across formats (email, blog, social media)

Blaze

Speed up your marketing content—fuel your growth with AI.

What it is:
Blaze.ai is an AI-powered content creation tool for marketers and growth-focused businesses. It helps you generate high-converting copy for emails, landing pages, ads, blog posts, and more—tailored to your brand and optimized for performance.

Why it's powerful for businesses:

- **Marketing-focused templates:** Blaze.ai is designed with growth in mind, offering templates for cold outreach, PPC ads, product descriptions, and SEO articles.
- **Personalized AI output:** Unlike generic AI tools, Blaze lets you train the model to reflect your tone of voice and audience preferences.
- **Built-in workflows:** Create multi-touch campaigns quickly with suggested sequences and integrated tools for planning and scheduling content.
- **SEO assistance:** Generates keyword-optimized blog posts and on-page SEO content to boost visibility and organic traffic.
- **Designed for scale:** Ideal for solopreneurs, agencies, and marketing teams looking to publish more without sacrificing quality.

Best use cases for businesses:

- **Accelerate email marketing** with high-performing cold emails and follow-ups
- **Test landing page variations** fast to improve conversions
- **Generate blog content** at scale to grow your SEO footprint
- **Support your sales team** with AI-crafted scripts, proposals, and outreach copy

---

Apollo.io

Find leads. Engage smarter. Grow faster.

What it is:
Apollo.io is a powerful all-in-one sales intelligence platform that helps businesses find verified B2B contacts, enrich their CRM data, and automate multichannel outreach. It's designed to help sales teams and business owners generate more pipeline with less manual effort.

Why it's powerful for businesses:

- **Massive lead database:** Access over 275 million verified contacts with advanced filters like job title, tech stack, funding, and intent signals.
- **Outbound automation:** Build and launch personalized cold email sequences, LinkedIn outreach, and calling cadences—all in one place.
- **CRM enrichment:** Automatically clean, enrich, and sync your CRM with accurate, real-time data so your team always works from the most current info.
- **AI-powered writing tools:** Apollo's AI helps you craft tailored messages based on persona, industry, and recent activity.
- **Revenue intelligence:** Track performance metrics, email engagement, and deal progression to continuously optimize your outbound motion.

Best use cases for businesses:

- **Fuel outbound sales** with verified contacts and multi-touch cadences
- **Keep your CRM accurate** and synced with fresh B2B data
- **Launch and test outbound campaigns** at scale without bloated tech stacks

- **Empower marketing and SDRs** to collaborate using data-driven insights and AI-generated content

---

ElevenLabs

Create Podcasts. Dub Audio and Add AI Voiceovers. Build an AI Conversational Agent.

What it is:

ElevenLabs is a cutting-edge voice AI platform that enables businesses to create ultra-realistic speech using AI-generated or custom-cloned voices. It's designed to bring human-like conversation to chatbots, virtual assistants, training modules, and voice-driven content, making interactions more engaging, branded, and scalable.

Why it's powerful for businesses:

- **Hyper-realistic voice synthesis:** Generate speech that sounds natural, emotional, and tailored to your brand voice, far beyond robotic text-to-speech.
- **Conversational AI-ready:** Integrate with GPT-powered chatbots or assistants to create lifelike, two-way voice conversations across support, sales, or onboarding.
- **Custom voice cloning:** Create and deploy your own AI voice for product walkthroughs, branded assistants, or internal training—instantly scalable across channels.
- **Multilingual capabilities:** Reach global audiences with AI voices that fluently speak over 20 languages, ideal for localization and international support.
- **Real-time API:** Build dynamic voice experiences into your app, website, or smart device with low-latency streaming support.

Best use cases for businesses:

- **Create voice-powered chatbots and AI assistants** that sound human and empathetic
- **Deliver branded audio experiences** for onboarding, training, or help centers
- **Voice-enable your product or platform** with multilingual support
- **Produce scalable video content** with AI narration for marketing, education, or customer service
- **Clone your founder's or brand ambassador's voice** for consistent messaging at scale

Chapter Takeaway

Stop thinking about "sales" and "marketing." Start thinking about your "revenue engine." Success in today's market requires a holistic approach where human alignment and powerful technology work in perfect harmony. By defining clear roles, fostering deep collaboration, and supercharging your unified team with the right AI tools, you can finally stop sputtering and build an engine that drives predictable, explosive growth.

Chapter 12

Your Marketing Workout Plan: Building the Muscle for Growth

Let's get one thing straight: if your marketing approach is to just "dabble"—posting here and there, trying a few random tactics without a plan—you're wasting your time. It's like going to the gym once, lifting a single dumbbell, and expecting six-pack abs. It doesn't work.

Like any endeavor that yields real results, effective marketing requires a serious commitment of one of two key resources: **time or money.** You either commit your own time to be focused, strategic, and consistent, or you invest in someone else to do it for you. There is no magic in-between if you want to actually grow.

Worried you don't have thousands of dollars a month to invest? That's okay. It just means you're starting with a DIY "bodyweight" routine for now. The key isn't the size of your budget; it's the focus and consistency of your effort. This chapter is your workout plan.

The Game Plan: Understanding the Customer Journey

Before you start any workout, you need to know the course. In marketing, that course is the **sales funnel**. It's the path a stranger takes to become a loyal customer, and it generally has three stages:

1. **Awareness (Top of Funnel):** The "I didn't know you existed" stage. Your goal here is to get noticed and capture attention.
2. **Consideration (Middle of Funnel):** The "Hmm, this is interesting, tell me more" stage. Your goal is to build trust and demonstrate your expertise by providing valuable information—blog posts, how-to videos, detailed guides—that helps them solve their problem.
3. **Conversion (Bottom of Funnel):** The "Okay, I'm ready to buy" stage. Your goal is to make it easy and compelling for them to take action with clear offers and a simple purchase process.

Your marketing plan needs "exercises" that address every stage of this journey.

Your Core Exercises: The Modern Marketing Mix

A balanced workout plan combines different types of exercises. Your marketing plan should do the same. Here are the three core disciplines.

1. SEO (Search Engine Optimization): Your Long-Term Strength Training Think of SEO as building foundational muscle. It's not flashy, you don't see results overnight, and it requires consistent effort. But over time, it builds the organic strength that makes you a powerhouse. The goal is to optimize your website so that when someone searches on Google for a problem you solve, you show up at the top of the results.

- **Key Lifts:** Keyword Research (finding the terms your customers use), On-Page Optimization (making your site easy for Google to read), Content Creation (writing useful articles that answer customer questions), and Link Building (getting other reputable sites to link to you, like a vote of confidence).
- **Essential Gear:** Google Analytics, Google Keyword Planner, SEMrush, Ahrefs, Yoast SEO (for WordPress).

2. PPC (Pay-Per-Click): Your High-Intensity Interval Training (HIIT)
PPC is your way to buy speed. It's the intense workout that gets you fast, targeted results. You pay Google or social media platforms to place your ad directly in front of potential customers *right now*. It costs money for every click, but it's the fastest way to get traffic and test offers.

- **Key Lifts:** Keyword Selection (bidding on the right search terms), Compelling Ad Copy (writing ads people actually want to click), Landing Page Optimization (making sure the page they land on is clear and persuasive), and A/B Testing (constantly testing different ads to see what works best).
- **Essential Gear:** Google Ads, AdEspresso, SEMrush (for checking out the competition).

3. Social Media Marketing: Your Community & Flexibility Work
Social media is where your brand shows its personality. It's less about brute strength or pure speed and more about building relationships, engaging in conversations, and staying flexible. It's your "active recovery" and community-building day.

- **Key Lifts:** Platform Selection (don't be everywhere; be where your customers are), Content Strategy (a mix of promotions, education, and behind-the-scenes content), and Community

Engagement (actually talking to people in the comments and messages!).
- **Essential Gear:** Hootsuite or Buffer (for scheduling), Canva (for creating visuals).

Putting It All Together: The Cohesive Strategy

You wouldn't go to the gym and *only* work on your left bicep. A good routine is balanced. The same goes for marketing. SEO, PPC, and social media should work in harmony.

- **Consistent Branding:** Your "look" (logos, colors) and "voice" (tone) should be the same everywhere to build recognition and trust.
- **Integrated Campaigns:** A new product launch shouldn't just be a PPC ad. It should be a blog post (SEO), a series of social media teasers (Social), and a targeted ad campaign (PPC), all working together to create buzz.

This is where strategy separates the amateurs from the pros. I saw this firsthand with a client of mine—a fantastic local heat and air (HVAC) company.

Case Study: From Wasted Spend to 400% Growth

The "Before" State: The HVAC company was working with the digital marketing arm of the Yellow Pages. This agency's approach to online marketing was stuck in the past; they treated it just like their old print advertising, with a "set it and forget it" mentality. As a result, the client had almost no online traffic, no meaningful customer engagement, and virtually zero sales coming from their website. They were spending money every month with nothing to show for it.

The Key Actions: When my company came in, we didn't just tweak their ads; we scrapped the old, broken approach entirely. We built a comprehensive digital marketing strategy from the ground up, designed specifically to achieve their core business goals: more phone calls from qualified local customers and more online bookings. This involved a cohesive mix of local SEO, targeted PPC ads, and a content strategy that answered the real questions their customers were asking.

The "After" State: The results were dramatic. By implementing a modern, strategic "workout plan," the client received a **400% increase in relevant website traffic** from their target geographical area. More importantly, they achieved this while **spending 25% less per month** than they had been paying their previous agency. They stopped wasting money on a strategy that didn't work and reinvested a smaller amount into a plan that delivered tangible, measurable results.

Tracking Your Gains: Measuring What Matters

The only way to know if your workout is effective is to track your progress. The same is true for marketing. You must measure your activities to see what's working and what's a waste of time and money.

- **Key Metrics to Watch:**
    - **Clicks & Traffic:** Are people seeing your message and coming to your site?
    - **Engagement:** Are they commenting, sharing, and interacting with your content?
    - **Leads & Phone Calls:** Are they taking the next step and showing real interest?
    - **Conversion Rate:** Of the people who show interest, how many are actually buying? This is the most important metric.

- **Analyze and Adapt:** Use tools like Google Analytics to see which channels are driving the most traffic and sales. If your social media efforts are generating lots of engagement but no sales, while your SEO-driven blog posts are converting like crazy, it's time to adjust your "workout plan." Double down on what works, and either fix or drop what doesn't.

Chapter Takeaway

Your marketing mix is your business's fitness routine. Dabbling gets you nowhere. Consistency is everything. By creating a balanced plan that combines the long-term strength of SEO, the speed of PPC, and the relationship-building of social media, you build a powerful and resilient marketing engine. And just like fitness, the online world changes constantly, so staying informed, tracking your progress, and being willing to adapt is what keeps your marketing in top shape.

Chapter 13

Stop Doing Junk Reps: Sales Activities That Actually Drive Outcomes

Sales teams are the lifeblood of your business—they drive revenue, build client relationships, and keep the wheels turning. But sometimes, instead of closing deals, they're stuck doing tasks that make them *look* busy without actually moving the needle.

You know the ones:

- Updating the CRM for the third time today... just in case.
- Making 50 calls on an out-of-date list to meet a call quota.
- Attending a "quick sync" meeting that spirals into a two-hour TED Talk.

- Color-coding a pipeline spreadsheet no one will ever open again.
- Logging every call, email, sneeze, and thought into five different platforms.

These activities are the sales equivalent of **junk reps** at the gym. They involve movement, they take time, and they make you feel like you're working, but they don't build any real muscle. They are activities without outcomes.

I learned this lesson under fire while working for a large corporate company. The management culture wasn't just focused on activity; they were obsessed with dictating process. Leaders with no fundamental understanding of the sales workflow would select new software and mandate new techniques they knew nothing about, all in the name of "improving" our performance.

The pressure was immense. The focus was entirely on hitting arbitrary numbers—calls made, emails sent—regardless of whether they led to anything. To make matters more complicated, I knew I had been hired at a slightly higher hourly rate than many of my colleagues, including my direct supervisor. This information was supposed to be secret, but it hung over me. I felt a constant, grinding need to justify my worth by working my socks off, even if the work itself was pointless.

I watched my colleagues burn out trying to hit these nonsensical activity quotas. So I made a different choice. I decided to focus exclusively on outcomes and quality. While others were frantically making calls to dead numbers to hit their quota, I spent my time researching fewer, better prospects. While they were logging useless data into a clunky new software, I was crafting personalized emails that actually got a response.

In the end, while still navigating the corporate mandates, I delivered higher quality results and ultimately greater numbers than my colleagues. It was a powerful lesson: the system was designed to reward the appearance of work, but the market only ever rewards results. My time there taught me that a leader's job isn't to dictate a process they don't understand; it's to clear the path of junk reps and empower their team to focus on the real work of selling.

The real magic happens when salespeople are focused on one thing: **selling**. It's time to eliminate the junk reps and design a workout plan that builds real strength.

The Master Trainer's Mindset: Shift from Activity to Outcome

Your first job as a leader is to change how you measure success. Stop rewarding junk reps. A salesperson who makes 100 calls and schedules one meeting is not more productive than one who makes 20 calls and schedules five meetings.

- **Kill Useless Metrics:** Throw out any metric that measures activity for activity's sake. Call quotas, number of emails sent, hours logged in the CRM—these are mostly vanity metrics.
- **Measure What Matters:** Replace them with outcome-based metrics. Track the number of *qualified* meetings scheduled, the value of new pipeline created, the sales cycle length, and—most importantly—the deals closed.
- **Ask Your Team:** Your salespeople know which tasks are pointless. Create a safe environment where they can tell you, "This report takes me two hours every Friday and I don't think anyone reads it." Listen to them. They are your best source for identifying waste.

The Core Lifts: Effective Sales Techniques

Once you've cleared away the junk, you can focus your team's training on the powerful, muscle-building exercises that actually win deals. There are two fundamental "lifts" every salesperson must master.

1. Active Listening: The Foundational Exercise This is the most critical and most underrated skill in sales. It's the ability to stop talking, stop planning your next sentence, and truly *hear* what a client is saying—and what they're *not* saying. A salesperson who masters active listening can identify a client's true needs, fears, and motivations, allowing them to tailor a solution perfectly.

- **How to Train It:** Use role-playing exercises in your team meetings. One person plays the client with a specific problem, the other plays the salesperson. After, give feedback specifically on the listening. Did they interrupt? Did they ask clarifying questions? Did they understand the client's core problem, or just hear the surface-level request?

2. Consultative Selling: The Powerlift This is the shift from being a "product pitcher" to being a "problem solver." A traditional salesperson shows up and talks about their product's features. A consultative salesperson shows up and asks about the client's business challenges. They act like a trusted advisor, not a vendor.

- **How to Train It:** Teach your team to lead with questions, not statements. Instead of, "Let me tell you about our amazing software," they should be asking, "What are the biggest efficiency challenges your team is facing right now?" This approach builds immediate trust and makes the eventual product pitch feel like a helpful solution, not an unsolicited ad. By focusing on the client's needs, your team will naturally prioritize high-quality conversations over a high quantity of junk calls.

Building the Right "Gym" Culture

Great techniques only stick if they're supported by the right environment. Your job as a leader is to build a sales culture that values outcomes and continuous improvement.

- **Celebrate the Wins, Not Just the Work:** When you give shout-outs, don't praise the person who "made the most calls." Praise the person who spent two weeks nurturing a difficult lead and finally landed a huge meeting. You're signaling to the entire team what real success looks like.
- **Become a Coach, Not a Scorekeeper:** Your regular check-ins shouldn't just be about reviewing the numbers. They should be coaching sessions. "I see you're struggling to get past gatekeepers. Let's role-play a few approaches." or "That was a fantastic discovery call. What did you learn that the rest of the team could use?"
- **Monitor Progress and Stay Agile:** Continuously monitor your outcome-based metrics. If you see that a new approach isn't working, be willing to adjust. The market is always changing, and your sales strategy needs to be able to adapt with it.

Chapter Takeaway

Sales success isn't about just working hard; it's about working smart. It comes from ditching the "junk reps" and focusing on the activities that build real muscle: forging genuine relationships through active listening and consultative selling. As a leader, your role is to be the master trainer—to design the right workout plan, provide the right coaching, and create a culture that celebrates real results, not just the appearance of being busy.

Chapter 14

The Smart Outreach Engine: Harnessing AI for Growth

Of course. This chapter dives into one of the most timely and crucial topics for any modern leader: Artificial Intelligence. The original draft is full of excellent, practical information on everything from the philosophy of AI to the specific steps for creating an outreach program. It also has some of the best, most personality-filled lines in the manuscript so far.

My revision's primary goal was to take all these valuable but separate pieces and forge them into a single, cohesive, and actionable playbook. I've structured it as a step-by-step guide to **building your own AI-powered outreach engine**, preserving your best lines and injecting that same energy throughout the entire chapter.

Revised: Chapter 11 - The Smart Outreach Engine: Harnessing AI for Growth

Let's talk about AI. For a long time, I thought it was mainly hype—something for tech geeks or billion-dollar companies. But after experimenting with a host of tools, I realized this stuff actually works. Well, some of it!

Many leaders are paralyzed by two big questions about AI: "Will it take my team's jobs?" and "Where do I even start?"

Let's clear the air. AI isn't here to replace your skilled people. In my opinion, AI is a superpower for those who already have skills in design, sales, or process management. It's a tool that automates the grunt work, freeing up your team to be more strategic and creative. It's the difference between digging a ditch with a spoon and using an excavator.

As for where to start? You start by building an engine. This chapter is your guide to building a smart, AI-powered outreach and lead generation engine, step-by-step.

Step 1: The Fuel — Defining Your Target with AI's Help

An engine is useless without the right fuel. In outreach, your fuel is a crystal-clear understanding of your target audience. Feeding bad data or a vague audience profile into an AI system is like asking a Magic 8-Ball for financial advice—it'll give you an answer, but you probably shouldn't bet the business on it.

Your goal is to find the people who are actually interested in what you're selling.

- **Start with the Basics:** Use your existing data to define your ideal customer's demographics (age, location, income) and psychographics (values, interests, lifestyle). Create a few detailed "buyer personas" that feel like real people.
- **Let AI Find the Patterns:** This is where AI gives you a leg up. Tools like Google Analytics can analyze your website traffic and customer data to spot hidden patterns. Which blog posts do your best customers read? Where do they drop off in the checkout process? AI can give you these actionable insights without you needing a data science degree.
- **Listen at Scale:** Use AI-powered social listening tools to understand what your target audience is talking about online. What are their biggest frustrations? What solutions are they

searching for? This helps you craft messaging that speaks their language.

Step 2: Building the Engine — Your AI-Powered Lead Generation System

Once you know who you're targeting, you can build the engine that finds and qualifies them at scale. This is where AI moves from analysis to action.

An AI-driven lead generation system uses data and predictive modeling to do the heavy lifting that used to take sales teams hundreds of hours.

- **Data Analysis:** The AI system analyzes data from your website, social media, and CRM to identify visitor behaviors that signal interest.
- **Predictive Modeling:** Based on the behavior of your past customers, the AI predicts which *new* leads are most likely to convert. It learns what a high-quality lead looks like for your business.
- **Automated Lead Scoring:** Instead of your sales team manually sifting through a giant list, the AI automatically scores every lead based on their potential. A visitor who downloaded a pricing sheet gets a high score; someone who just read one blog post gets a lower score.

This system streamlines the top of your sales funnel, freeing your sales team from chasing cold leads so they can focus their energy on the hot prospects who are already interested and qualified.

Step 3: The Operating Manual — Running Your Outreach Program

You have the fuel and you've built the engine. Now it's time to run the plays. This is your operating manual for turning leads into customers, with AI assisting at every step.

1. **Personalize Your Outreach:** Use AI tools to draft personalized email campaigns and chatbot scripts that engage prospects at scale while still maintaining a human touch.
2. **Schedule and Attend Appointments:** Use AI scheduling tools to automatically book meetings with qualified leads, optimizing your calendar and eliminating back-and-forth emails.
3. **Clean Your Data (Constantly):** Dirty data is my pet peeve. An AI engine running on bad data is worthless. Use AI-powered solutions to regularly audit your database, removing duplicates and updating obsolete information. We'll cover this more in the next two chapters.
4. **Automate Proposals and Contracts:** Streamline your closing process with AI tools that generate customizable proposal and contract templates based on client needs, saving time and reducing errors.
5. **Fulfill Your Services:** Use AI-powered project management tools to track progress, assign tasks, and communicate status updates, ensuring you deliver what you promised consistently and on time.
6. **Maintain Communication:** Establish a routine for providing clients with monthly feedback. Use AI to help generate reports summarizing key metrics and insights, reinforcing your commitment to transparency.
7. **Never Stop Prospecting:** Your engine should always be running. Use AI to continuously identify new leads based on real-time data, keeping your pipeline full and staying ahead of the competition.

The goal is to create a harmonious partnership between your team and your technology. AI handles the scale and the data-sifting; your team provides the strategy, builds the relationships, and closes the deals.

Chapter Takeaway

Regularly review your business processes and ask a simple question: "Can a smart tool do this faster and better?" Streamlining routine tasks with AI not only boosts efficiency but also frees up your team to focus on the creative, strategic work that truly drives results. After all, if your team is still manually sorting spreadsheets in 2025, you might as well check if your office fax machine is also giving out relationship advice.

Chapter 15

The Second Sale: How to Turn Customers into Lifelong Fans

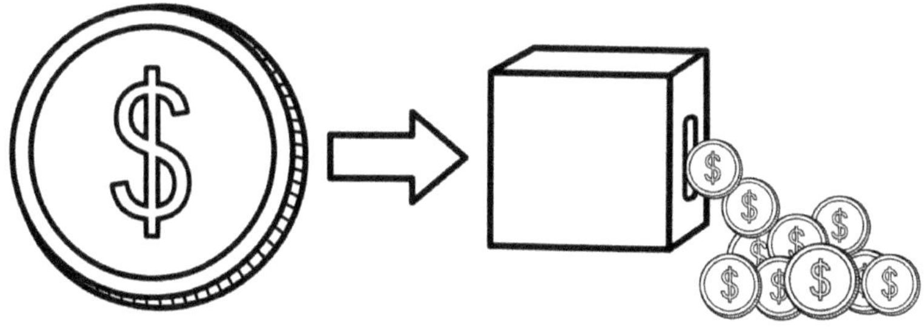

What if I told you that your most profitable new customer is the one you already have?

In the relentless hunt for growth, leaders often become obsessed with one thing: acquiring new customers. We spend fortunes on marketing, build complex sales funnels, and high-five every time a new name enters our CRM. This is the "first sale," and it's exhausting, expensive work.

But the smartest businesses know that the first sale isn't the end of the game; it's the beginning. The real, sustainable, and most profitable growth comes from the **"second sale."** The second sale is the ongoing process of earning your customer's loyalty, trust, and—most importantly—their future business. It's a shift from a "hunter" mindset to a "farmer" mindset. Instead of constantly chasing new prey, you cultivate the field you already have. And that field is a goldmine.

From Reactive Service to Proactive Success

Most companies have "customer service." This is the reactive, defensive part of the business. A customer has a problem, they call you, and you fix it. It's necessary, but it's a cost center. It doesn't generate growth; it just stops you from shrinking.

Elite companies build a "customer success" function. The goal of customer success isn't to fix problems; it's to ensure your customers achieve their desired outcome *using your product.* It's a proactive, strategic effort. A customer who truly succeeds with your product is a customer who is happy, loyal, and perfectly primed for the upsell.

Mining for Gold: Finding the Money in Your Portfolio

Let's be clear: focusing on existing customers is a direct revenue-generating strategy. This isn't just about being nice; it's about being profitable. This principle applies everywhere, and I saw it firsthand with one of my own clients.

One of my longest-standing clients is a nonprofit organization, and I have the honor of serving on their board. Initially, they hired my company for a specific, well-defined task: to handle their marketing. We could have simply fulfilled that contract and moved on.

However, because we were invested in their success, we focused on developing a thorough understanding of their organization. We listened to the challenges they were facing, including their staff issues, limited resources, and long-term vision. It became clear that their surface-level marketing problems were just a symptom of a larger operational issue—outdated, disconnected systems were holding them back.

Based on that insight, we went back to them with a proposal that went far beyond our original marketing work. We proposed designing and implementing a custom, cloud-based solution to address their fundamental organizational challenges.

The timing, in hindsight, was astonishing. We delivered the new system right before the COVID pandemic hit. While other organizations were scrambling to figure out how to operate remotely, our client seamlessly transitioned. Their new cloud infrastructure, which we built to solve a different set of problems, became their lifeline during a global crisis.

That single project, born from a deeper examination of an existing client's needs, not only proved incredibly valuable to them but also led to a much stronger professional relationship and a substantial economic benefit for my organization.

This is the power of the "second sale." It's about using the trust you've earned to look beyond the current contract and find the next, most valuable problem you can solve.

The Art of the Upsell (Without Being Sleazy) The key to a successful upsell is to frame it not as a pushy sales tactic, but as the next logical step in your customer's journey. You're not trying to squeeze more money out of them; you're guiding them to a better outcome.

- **The "Level Up" Offer:** A customer has been successfully using your basic accounting software for six months. Your CRM should trigger a note for your team to reach out. The conversation isn't, "Want to buy our more expensive version?" It's, "I see you've done a fantastic job organizing your finances with our starter plan. It looks like you're ready to take the next step. Our advanced module includes payroll and tax prep, which would solve the other challenges you mentioned when you first signed up."

- **The "Adjacent Solution" Cross-Sell:** "Since you love our running shoes, have you seen our moisture-wicking socks specifically designed to prevent the blisters you mentioned in your last review?" It's a helpful, logical suggestion that enhances the value of their original purchase.

Trying to upsell a brand-new, confused customer is like asking someone for a second date while you're still on the first one and have just spilled wine on them. The timing is all wrong. The perfect moment for the upsell is *after* they have already experienced a win with your product. Your CRM is your treasure map here, using purchase history and usage data to tell you exactly when that moment is.

Creating Raving Fans: Your Volunteer Marketing Department

The ultimate goal of the second sale is to turn your happy customers into a passionate, commission-free sales and marketing team.

- **Build Your Feedback Engine:** Stop waiting for customers to complain. Systematically ask for their feedback through surveys, check-in calls, and reviews. A glowing testimonial from a real customer is more credible and powerful than any advertisement you could ever write. Feature those testimonials everywhere.
- **Launch a Referral Program:** Make it incredibly easy and rewarding for happy customers to bring you new ones. Offer them a discount, a gift card, or an exclusive feature for every new customer they refer. They are already telling their friends about you; you might as well formalize the process and reward them for it.

- **Foster a Community:** Create a space where your best customers can connect with each other. This could be a private Facebook group, a Slack channel, or a series of exclusive webinars. When customers start answering each other's questions and sharing their own success stories, their loyalty shifts from being transactional to being deeply tribal. They no longer just use your product; they belong to your brand.

Chapter Takeaway

The relentless, expensive chase for new customers is a hamster wheel. The smartest way to grow your business is to turn your attention inward. Obsess over the customers you already have. Help them win. Guide them to the next logical step. Empower them to tell your story. When you master the art of the second sale, you don't just create a sustainable business—you build an army of loyal fans who will grow it for you.

Chapter 16

Your Business's Brain: Mastering Your CRM and Data

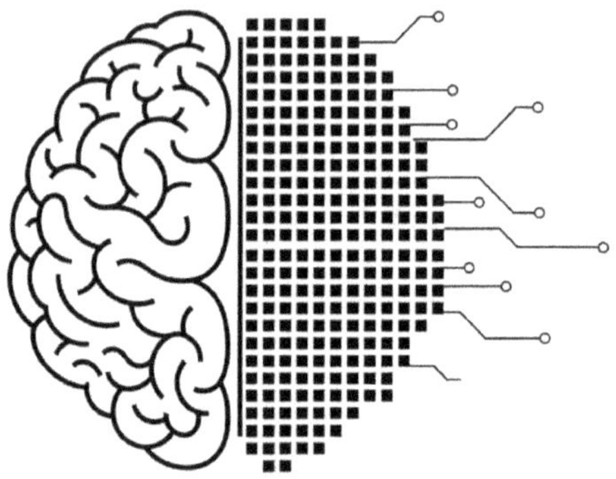

Does your business suffer from amnesia?

Here's the test: a customer calls your support line with an issue. Does your support agent know that this same customer just bought a major product from your sales team last week? Do they know that they clicked on a marketing email yesterday?

If the answer is no, then each department is treating that customer like a total stranger. This is business amnesia, and it's frustrating for your customers and disastrous for your bottom line.

The cure is a Customer Relationship Management (CRM) system. But don't think of it as just software. Think of it as your business's **central nervous system.** It's the brain that remembers every interaction and the network that connects all the limbs—sales, marketing, and service—so they can work together as one intelligent organism.

The Basic Function: Building a Perfect Memory

At its core, a CRM solves the amnesia problem. It is a single source of truth that records every touchpoint in a customer's journey:

- Every email they've opened.
- Every sales call they've had.
- Every product they've purchased.
- Every support ticket they've filed.

With all this information in one place, any team member can quickly understand a customer's entire history. This consistency builds trust and makes your business look smart and coordinated, not forgetful and chaotic.

Advanced Function 1: The Charming Robot Butler (Automation)

Once your CRM has a memory, you can teach it to perform tasks automatically. This is your "charming robot butler," working 24/7 to create helpful, timely, and personalized experiences for your customers without you lifting a finger.

Instant Gratification: Answering Questions 24/7 When a customer has a question, they want an answer *now*. They don't want to wait hours or days for a response. Your robot butler is always on duty, providing instant feedback that dramatically improves the customer experience.

- **Address Common Questions:** Many of the inquiries you receive are repetitive: "What are your hours?" "What is your return policy?" "Do you ship internationally?" You can program your automated system with a database of clear, accurate answers to these FAQs, freeing up your human team for more complex issues.
- **Guide Customers to Resources:** Sometimes an answer isn't enough. An automated system can act as a helpful guide, directing customers to other useful resources. If a customer asks about troubleshooting a product, the system can respond with a direct link to a video tutorial or a detailed knowledge base article, providing a much richer level of support.

Proactive Engagement: Nurturing Leads and Customers Automation isn't just about reacting; it's about proactively engaging.

- **The Instant "Thank You":** When a customer makes a purchase, they immediately get a thank-you email. This simple act confirms the order and makes them feel appreciated.
- **The Helpful Follow-Up:** A week after someone buys a new camera, they automatically get an email with a link to a "Beginner's Guide to Photography" video. This adds value beyond the sale and builds trust.
- **The Gentle Nudge:** If a potential client viewed your pricing page but didn't book a call, they might get a friendly email a few days later asking if they have any questions. This re-engages their interest at a critical moment.

How to Implement It Effectively An automated system is only as smart as you make it. Start by identifying the most common customer inquiries. Create a comprehensive database of answers and resources. Most importantly, don't "set it and forget it."

Continuously monitor the interactions and use customer feedback to refine the responses. A good robot butler is always learning.

Advanced Function 2: The Crystal Ball (Upselling and Personalization)

This is where the magic happens. By analyzing the data in your CRM, you can move from reacting to a customer's past to *predicting* their future needs. Your CRM becomes your crystal ball.

- **Identify Upselling Opportunities:** By segmenting customers based on their purchase history, you can identify perfect upselling opportunities. The CRM can automatically flag customers who bought "Product A" as prime candidates for "Product B" and alert your sales team. A customer who frequently buys fitness gear can be placed in a "premium" segment to receive targeted offers for high-end equipment.
- **Create Deeply Personalized Experiences:** Integrate data from all your platforms—sales, marketing, social media, support—to get a complete 360-degree view of your customer. This holistic perspective allows you to build real, long-term relationships.
  - **Tailor Your Service:** A coffee shop could use its CRM to remember a regular's favorite drink and suggest it upon their next visit. This small detail creates a powerful feeling of recognition and loyalty.
  - **Gather Feedback:** Use your CRM to automatically solicit customer opinions through surveys after a purchase or service interaction. This shows customers you value their opinion and provides you with invaluable data to improve your business.
  - **Acknowledge Milestones:** A simple, automated "Happy Birthday" email with a special discount can make a customer feel special and keep your brand top-of-mind.

Choosing Your System: The Practical Guide

Selecting a CRM is like choosing an operating system for your business's brain. It's a critical decision. Most platforms offer a free trial, so test them out before committing. Here are some of the top-rated systems, known for their features, ease of use, and support.

- **Salesforce:** The industry giant. Incredibly powerful and customizable, with advanced reporting and analytics. Best for larger teams with complex needs. *(Starts at approx. $25/user/month)*
- **HubSpot CRM:** Famously user-friendly with fantastic email tracking and lead management. Its free version is one of the best on the market, making it a great starting point for any business. *(Premium plans start around $50/user/month)*
- **Zoho CRM:** A strong all-rounder that offers great value, with solid workflow automation and social media integration. *(Starts at approx. $12/user/month)*
- **Pipedrive:** Designed by salespeople, for salespeople. Its visual sales pipeline management is intuitive and helps teams stay focused on activities that close deals. *(Starts at approx. $15/user/month)*
- **Microsoft Dynamics 365:** A powerful choice for businesses already invested in the Microsoft ecosystem, offering excellent AI-driven insights and deep integration with Office 365 and other Microsoft tools. *(Starts at approx. $65/user/month)*

Chapter Takeaway

Using a CRM system is like giving your business a crystal ball, minus the weird smoke and dramatic music. As customer needs evolve faster than fashion trends, a well-tuned CRM helps you keep up, stand out, and stay sane. From upselling without being pushy, to automating follow-ups like a charming robot butler, to turning data into delightful customer experiences, a good CRM isn't just helpful—it's your secret weapon. Nail it, and you're not just keeping customers—you're practically adopting them.

Chapter 17

Don't Bake with Salt Instead of Sugar: The Leader's Guide to Clean Data

Making a business decision with dirty data is like baking a cake with salt instead of sugar. No matter how good your recipe (your strategy) is, no matter how skilled y our bakers (your team) are, the result will be a disaster you'll have to force down with a smile.

In business, your data is your most fundamental ingredient. If it's inaccurate, outdated, or just plain wrong, then every strategy you build, every marketing campaign you launch, and every sales forecast you make is built on shaky ground. It's time to stop guessing and start cleaning out the pantry.

What is Dirty Data? (Identifying the Contaminants)

"Dirty data" isn't some abstract technical term. It's a collection of specific contaminants that spoil your results. It's my pet peeve because it's an unforced error that sabotages even the best teams. Look for these culprits in your systems:

- **Duplicates:** The same customer entered into your CRM five times with five slightly different spellings of their name. This completely skews your customer count and makes your team look disorganized.

- **Outdated Information:** Contact records for people who left their job three years ago. Following up on these leads isn't just a waste of time; it's embarrassing.
- **Inaccurate or Incomplete Entries:** Phone numbers with missing digits, email addresses with typos, and blank fields where critical information should be.
- **Inconsistent Formats:** Some addresses say "Street," others say "St." Some states are abbreviated ("OK"), others are spelled out ("Oklahoma"). This makes it impossible to accurately sort, filter, or analyze your data.

This contamination seeps in from everywhere: simple human typos during data entry, errors during a system migration, or data rot from old, legacy systems.

The High Cost of a Contaminated Kitchen

Why should you, as a leader, be obsessed with this? Because dirty data costs you real money and credibility. It wastes marketing spend, frustrates sales teams, creates embarrassing customer experiences, and leads to disastrous strategic decisions.

I've seen this happen with multiple clients who suffer from a "data hoarding" mentality. They have massive databases or CRM systems filled with tens of thousands of contacts and take pride in the sheer volume. But when you look closer, it's a digital junkyard.

Case Study: The Courage to Declare Data Bankruptcy

The "Before" State: A client had a huge CRM database that they believed was a major asset. In reality, it was filled with what I call "dirty data"—contacts that were massively out of date, unverified for years, and totally useless for any positive outcome. The sales team was terrified to even use it because every call was a disconnected number and every email was a bounce-back. It was a swamp of bad information that was creating more work than value.

The Key Action: The leadership team had to make a courageous decision. They had to acknowledge that this data they had been clinging to had no real worth. It felt like throwing away an asset, but in reality, they were throwing away trash. We established a new rule: all data must be either a) actively verified and updated, or b) deleted. There was no in-between.

The "After" State: They essentially declared "data bankruptcy" on their old, useless records and started fresh with a smaller, but pristine, set of data. The sales team was re-energized. Now, every contact in their CRM was a verified, potential lead. Their outreach became dramatically more effective, their morale skyrocketed, and they started activating new clients because they were finally working with clean, reliable ingredients.

The Deep Clean: Your Data Hygiene Playbook

Treating your data like a critical asset starts with a deep clean. This isn't just a job for your IT department; it's a strategic initiative you must lead. Here are the three core techniques.

1. **Deduplication (One Entry Per Customer):** Your goal is a single, unified record for each customer. Use software tools, often built into your CRM, to automatically scan your databases for duplicate entries. Set clear rules for what constitutes a duplicate (e.g., a matching email address and last name) and merge the records into one "golden record."
2. **Standardization (A Common Language):** Decide on a single, consistent format for all your data fields and enforce it. "Street" or "St."? Pick one. Two-letter state codes or the full name? Pick one. This ensures that when you filter or sort your data, you get

accurate results every time. This needs to be a clear policy for anyone entering data.

3. **Validation (The Quality Check):** This is your real-time contamination prevention. Implement validation rules in your data entry forms. For example, a phone number field should only accept numbers and have a specific digit count. An email field should require an "@" symbol. This prevents bad data from ever getting into your system in the first place.

Keeping the Kitchen Clean: Making Hygiene a Habit

A deep clean is great, but a pristine kitchen gets messy again after one meal if you don't maintain it. Data hygiene is not a one-time project; it's a continuous process.

- **Schedule Regular Audits:** Just like financial books, your data needs to be audited periodically. Set a quarterly schedule to review your data for accuracy and consistency.
- **Cycle Out Old Data:** Don't be a data hoarder. Records for customers who haven't engaged with you in several years are likely outdated and are just cluttering your system. Create a policy to regularly archive or delete these "deprecated" records.
- **Create a Culture of Accuracy:** Train your team on the importance of data quality. Explain *why* it matters to their jobs and to the company's success. When your team understands that clean data helps them perform better and earn more, they become active partners in keeping it clean.

Chapter Takeaway

Your data is the most critical ingredient in your business. Leading with a contaminated pantry is a recipe for failure. As a leader, you must champion the cause of data hygiene, transforming it from a back-end technical chore into a core strategic priority. Clean data builds trust, saves money, and empowers your team to make smart, confident decisions that drive real growth.

Chapter 18

Know Your Numbers:

A Leader's No-BS Guide to Financial Health

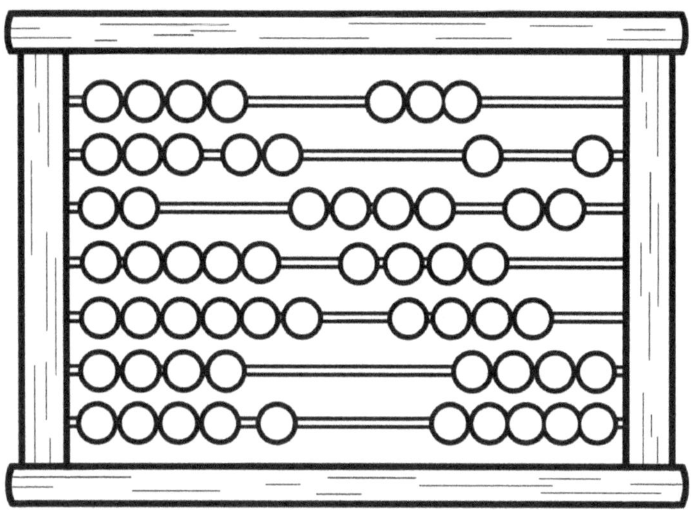

Let's be honest. For many brilliant leaders, the moment someone pulls out a financial statement, their eyes glaze over. It's a sea of debits, credits, and acronyms that feels intentionally confusing—a secret language designed by accountants to make everyone else feel dumb.

But flying blind on your financials is one of the fastest ways to crash your business. You don't need to be a CPA, but you absolutely must understand the story your numbers are telling you. Not knowing your numbers is like a ship's captain not knowing how to read a compass. You might be a great leader, but you're still lost at sea.

This is your no-BS guide to financial literacy. We're going to strip away the jargon and focus on the three vital signs of your business's health.

The Three Vital Signs: Your Business's Health Checkup

There are three core financial statements. Each one answers a different, critical question. Think of them like a doctor's report.

1. **The Profit & Loss (P&L) Statement:** Answers "Are we making money?"
2. **The Balance Sheet:** Answers "What is our net worth?"
3. **The Cash Flow Statement:** Answers "Where did the cash actually go?"

Let's break them down.

Vital Sign #1: The Profit & Loss Statement (Are We Winning or Losing?)

The P&L (also called an Income Statement) is y our company's report card for a specific period—a month, a quarter, or a year. It's a simple story of what you earned versus what you spent.

Its formula is dead simple: **Revenue - Expenses = Profit (or Loss)**

It tells you if you won or lost the game during that period. Here is a super-simplified example:

Simplified P&L Statement (For Q3)

Revenue (Money from sales) | $100,000

Less: Cost of Goods Sold (COGS) | -$30,000

Gross Profit | **$70,000**

Less: Operating Expenses (Salaries, rent, marketing) | -$50,000

Net Profit (or Income) | $20,000 |

If this number is positive, congratulations, you were profitable for the quarter! If it's negative, you had a net loss. The P&L is the first place you should look to understand your company's basic performance.

Vital Sign #2: The Balance Sheet (What Are We Worth?)

The Balance Sheet is different from the P&L. It's not a report card over time; it's a **snapshot** of your company's financial health on a *single day*. It answers the question: If we sold everything we own and paid off everything we owe, what would be left?

Its formula is the fundamental equation of accounting: **Assets = Liabilities + Equity**

- **Assets:** Everything your company *owns* that has value (cash, equipment, inventory).
- **Liabilities:** Everything your company *owes* to others (loans, supplier bills).
- **Equity:** The value left over for the owners. It's the difference between what you own and what you owe.

Here's a simplified look:

Simplified Balance Sheet (As of Sept. 30)

Assets | | Liabilities

Cash | $50,000 | Loans Payable | $60,000

Inventory | $40,000 | Accounts Payable | $20,000

Equipment | $30,000

Total Liabilities| $80,000

Total Assets | **$120,000** | **Owner's Equity** | **$40,000**

Total Liabilities + Equity | **$120,000**|

Notice how both sides balance? They must. This statement tells you the overall net worth and financial structure of your company.

Vital Sign #3: The Cash Flow Statement (Where Did the Money Go?)

This is the most important and most misunderstood statement of the three. A company can be profitable on its P&L but go bankrupt because it runs out of cash. This statement explains why.

The Cash Flow Statement is like your company's bank account statement. It doesn't care about "profit"; it only cares about one thing: **actual cash moving in and out of your business.**

Here's the crucial difference: Imagine you make a huge $50,000 sale to a client on December 30th, but they have 60 days to pay you.

- Your **P&L Statement** for the year looks amazing! It shows a $50,000 profit.
- But your **Cash Flow Statement** shows that zero cash has actually come into your bank account. You can't pay salaries with "profit"; you can only pay them with cash.

This is the "profit vs. cash flow" trap that sinks so many businesses. The Cash Flow Statement protects you by showing exactly how much cash you have and where it came from and went.

Simplified Cash Flow Statement (For Q3)

Cash from Operations (Day-to-day business) | $25,000

Cash from Investing (Buying/selling big assets) | -$10,000

Cash from Financing (Taking/paying back loans) | -$5,000

Net Increase/Decrease in Cash | $10,000

Beginning Cash Balance | $40,000

Ending Cash Balance| $50,000 |

This tells the real story of the cash in your business, which is the oxygen it needs to survive.

Chapter Takeaway

You don't need an MBA in finance to be a great leader, but you do need to speak the language of your business. Stop being intimidated by the numbers. By regularly reviewing these three vital signs—your P&L, your Balance Sheet, and, most importantly, your Cash Flow Statement—you can move from flying blind to making smart, data-driven decisions. Knowing your numbers isn't just about looking at the past; it's about confidently shaping your future.

Try This: The Leader's 15-Minute Financial Check-In

You don't need to live in spreadsheets, but you can't afford to be ignorant of your company's financial health. Block out 15 minutes on your calendar every single week for this check-in. Sit down with your bookkeeper, your key financial reports, or your dashboard and answer these three simple questions—one for each vital sign.

1. The Profit Question (from your P&L):

- "What was our single biggest unexpected expense this week/month? And what was our most surprisingly profitable product, service, or client?" *(This question forces you to look beyond the final profit number and understand the drivers behind it.)*

2. The Cash Question (from your Cash Flow / Bank Account):

- "How does our actual cash in the bank today compare to this time last month? Are any major payments from clients currently overdue?" *(This question focuses you on what matters most for survival: cash on hand.)*

3. The Worth Question (from your Balance Sheet):

- "Looking at our receivables and payables, are our clients paying us faster than we are paying our vendors, or is it the other way around?" *(This simple question gives you a powerful snapshot of your working capital and operational efficiency.)*

This simple, 15-minute weekly habit will do more for your financial literacy than a dozen textbooks. It moves you from being fearful of your financials to being in confident control of them.

Chapter 19

The Microscope and the Telescope

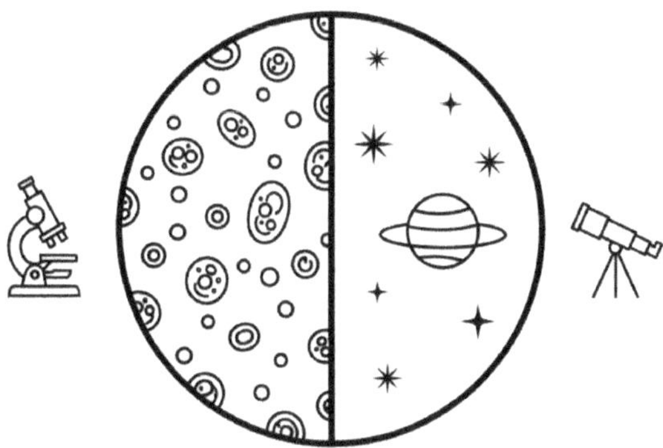

(This chapter focuses on the Micro vs. Macro Vision content)

We've all met the two kinds of dysfunctional leaders.

First, there's the **Micromanager.** They are lost in the weeds, obsessing over font choices on a presentation while the competition is eating their lunch. They check every email, question every decision, and drive their high-performing team insane because they can only see through a microscope.

Then there's the **Ivory Tower Dreamer.** They talk a big game about five-year plans and "synergistic paradigms," but they have no idea what's actually happening on the ground floor. Their grand strategies are completely disconnected from reality because they can only see through a telescope.

Both are failing. Effective leadership isn't about choosing one instrument. It's about knowing when to switch between the two.

The Microscope: Your Tool for Execution (Micro Vision)

The microscope is for examining the details of your daily operations. This is where you zoom in on the "how."

- **Performance Metrics:** Are sales numbers for a specific product trending up or down this week?
- **Customer Feedback:** What are the most common complaints your support team heard yesterday?
- **Workflow Efficiency:** Why does it take three days for a simple contract to get approved?

A leader who never uses the microscope becomes detached. They miss the small problems that, left unchecked, can grow into catastrophic failures. Regularly reviewing operational details and employee reports keeps you grounded in the reality of your business.

The Telescope: Your Tool for Strategy (Macro Vision)

The telescope is for looking at the big picture and the distant horizon. This is where you zoom out to see the "why" and "where."

- **Market Trends:** How is our industry changing? What new technologies are on the horizon?
- **Competitive Landscape:** What are our competitors doing, and where are they vulnerable?
- **Long-Term Goals:** Where do we want this company to be in three years? Are we on the right path to get there?

A leader who never uses the telescope is just reacting. They are steering the ship without a map, constantly surprised by the storms everyone else saw coming.

The Leader's Real Job: Master of the Switch

Your value as a leader isn't in your ability to use one tool well; it's in your ability to seamlessly switch between them. This is how you create a balanced and cohesive strategy.

- **Connect the "How" to the "Why":** You use the microscope to notice that customer response times are slow. You use the telescope to understand that this operational issue threatens your long-term strategic goal of being the market leader in customer satisfaction. The insight from one lens informs the action you take with the other.
- **Empower, Don't Hover:** The goal of the microscope is to diagnose problems, not to do your team's work for them. Once you've identified an issue, your job is to give your team the clear objective ("We need to reduce our average response time by 50%") and then trust them to figure out the best way to do it. This builds a culture of ownership and avoids the soul-crushing trap of micromanagement.
- **Foster a Two-Lens Culture:** Encourage your team to think with both lenses. During a team meeting, ask: "How does this daily task you're working on connect to our larger company goal of expanding into a new market?" This helps everyone see the bigger picture and makes their daily work more meaningful.

Chapter Takeaway

An effective leader is a master of perspective. They have the wisdom to use the telescope to set a bold, clear destination and the discipline to use the microscope to ensure the engine room is running flawlessly. By learning to switch between these two views, you can build a strong foundation for today while strategically navigating toward a successful tomorrow.

Chapter 20

Sailing into the Fog: A Leader's Guide to Uncertainty

In business, uncertainty isn't the exception; it's the norm. Markets shift, consumer behavior changes, new competitors emerge, and global events can rewrite your plans overnight.

A reactive leader gets caught in every storm, frantically bailing water and reacting to every wave. A proactive leader, however, treats uncertainty not as a crisis to be feared, but as a condition to be navigated. They don't pretend they can predict the future, but they prepare for it.

The Captain's Toolkit: How to Prepare for the Storm

Navigating through the fog requires the right set of tools to see what's coming and plan your route accordingly.

- **Your Radar (Risk Evaluation):** Before you even leave the harbor, you need to scan the horizon for potential threats.
    - **Market Volatility:** How stable is your market? Are you prepared for sudden drops in demand or increases in cost?
    - **Competitive Threats:** Who are your main competitors? What are their strengths? More importantly, where are they weak?
    - **Internal Gaps:** Do you have the right team, technology, and resources to handle a major challenge? A brutally honest internal audit is crucial.
- **Your Charts (Proactive Planning):** A good captain never has just one route.
    - **Flexible Strategies:** Your business plan should be a compass, not a straitjacket. Set clear objectives, but build in the flexibility to change course when the conditions demand it.
    - **Contingency Plans:** For your biggest risks, create specific "if-then" plans. "If our main supplier has a disruption, we will immediately switch to our vetted backup supplier." This turns panic into a calm, procedural response.
    - **Financial Reserves:** Maintain an emergency fund. Having cash reserves is the difference between weathering a storm and sinking in it.
- **Your Ship's Radio (Communication and Collaboration):** In a storm, silent leadership is failed leadership.
    - **Be Radically Transparent:** Keep your team informed about the challenges you're facing and the strategy for navigating them. This builds trust and eliminates the fear and rumor that thrive in a vacuum.

  - **Crowdsource Your Solutions:** Your crew on deck sees the waves up close. Create an environment where they feel safe to voice concerns and suggest solutions. The best idea for navigating the storm might come from your newest team member.

The Captain's Mindset: Embracing the Fog

The ultimate tool is your own mindset. You must foster a culture that sees uncertainty not as a threat, but as an opportunity.

- **Encourage Innovation:** The pressure of a challenge is often what sparks the most creative solutions. Give your team the freedom to experiment and explore new ways of doing things.
- **Reward Adaptability:** Celebrate team members who are flexible, resilient, and quick to pivot. Promote those who thrive in the fog, not just those who can execute a plan in calm seas.

Chapter Takeaway

You can't predict every storm, but with the right tech, data, and research, you don't have to. It's like sailing into choppy waters with radar, GPS, and a sturdy ship—sure, you'll still get splashed, but at least you won't capsize blindfolded. The future may be unpredictable, but preparation turns uncertainty into opportunity.

Chapter 21

The Art of the Win-Win: A Leader's Guide to Negotiation

Most people think negotiation is like arm wrestling—a tense, grunting contest of wills where one person wins and the other loses. They see it as a battle to be fought, a zero-sum game where every dollar in your pocket is a dollar out of theirs.

They're wrong.

Great negotiation isn't about beating the person across the table; it's about working *with* them to solve a problem. It's a process of creative collaboration, not combat. A bad negotiation leaves one party feeling cheated and damages the relationship. A great negotiation makes the pie bigger, so everyone gets a satisfying slice, and strengthens the relationship for the future.

As a leader, you are negotiating constantly, whether you realize it or not. You negotiate with new hires on salary, with vendors on pricing, with clients on contract terms, and even with other departments for resources. Mastering this skill is non-negotiable for your success.

The Mindset Shift: From Personal Discomfort to Professional Value

The single most important step in becoming a great negotiator happens before you say a single word. It's a mental shift. For many, this is the hardest part due to our own internal roadblocks.

I'll be honest—for years, I struggled with negotiations. Growing up in England, my family had very strict, unspoken rules about money: it was essential to have, but you must never, ever talk about it. Discussing finances was considered impolite, brash, and deeply uncomfortable.

This upbringing created a huge internal conflict for me in business. Every time I had to negotiate a contract or discuss pricing, it felt like I was breaking a sacred childhood rule. My gut instinct was to rush through it, to lowball my own value, to do anything to get the awkward "money talk" over with as quickly as possible. It was a terrible strategy, born from personal discomfort.

The breakthrough came when I learned to reframe the entire conversation. I had to force myself to stop thinking about it as *my* value or *my* money. The discussion isn't about your personal worth; it's about the objective **value** of the solution you bring to the table and the **return on investment (ROI)** the other party will receive.

By reflecting on the value I provide and focusing on the financial investment from a strategic, detached perspective, the conversation changes. It stops being a personal, impolite chat about money and becomes a professional, collaborative discussion about value. This mindset shift is the key to moving from an adversary to a partner.

Preparation is 90% of the Win

The outcome of a negotiation is determined long before you walk into the room. Amateurs show up and "wing it." Professionals show up prepared. Your prep work, grounded in that professional mindset, should focus on three key areas:

1. **Know Your Goal (and Your Walk-Away Point):** What is your ideal outcome? What is the absolute minimum you will accept? This bottom line is your "walk-away" point. Never, ever enter a

negotiation without knowing the precise point at which you will politely stand up and say, "I don't think we can reach an agreement here, but I appreciate your time." Having a clear walk-away point is the source of your confidence and power.

2. **Know** *Their* **Goal (The Most Overlooked Step):** Spend as much time thinking about what the other party wants as you do thinking about what you want. What are their underlying interests? What pressures are they under? Do they need to look good for their boss? Do they value speed and convenience over the absolute lowest price? The better you understand their needs, the more creative you can be in finding a solution that meets both your needs and theirs.
3. **Know Your Alternatives (Your BATNA):** In negotiation theory, this is called your **B**est **A**lternative **T**o a **N**egotiated **A**greement. In simple terms: what's your Plan B? If this deal completely falls apart, what is your next best option? Having a strong Plan B is liberating. It means you are not desperate. You can negotiate freely and confidently, knowing you'll be fine whether this specific deal works out or not.

In the Room: The Four Rules of the Game

Once you're prepared, the negotiation itself becomes a structured conversation. Follow these four rules to guide the process.

- **Rule #1: Separate the People from the Problem.** This is the golden rule. Be hard on the problem, but soft on the person. Even when you disagree strongly, maintain a tone of respect. Acknowledge their perspective before stating your own: *"I understand why you're proposing that price point, and it makes sense from your side. Let me walk you through the budget constraints we're facing on our end."* This simple act of validating their position defuses tension and makes them more receptive to yours.

- **Rule #2: Focus on Interests, Not Positions.** A "position" is *what* someone says they want ("I need a 10% discount"). An "interest" is the underlying *why* behind their demand ("I need to show my boss I controlled costs effectively"). If you can uncover their interest, you can often find creative ways to satisfy it without caving on their position. Perhaps instead of a discount, you can offer better payment terms, free implementation support, or an extended warranty—things that might be low-cost for you but high-value for them.
- **Rule #3: Invent Options for Mutual Gain.** Don't get trapped fighting over a single variable. The moment you feel like you're in a deadlock, it's time to get creative. Say, "Look, it seems like we're stuck on this point. Let's put it aside for a moment and brainstorm some other ways we could add value to this deal." The more options you have on the table, the more likely you are to find a unique combination that works for everyone.
- **Rule #4: Use Objective Criteria.** Whenever possible, base the discussion on fair, external standards—market rates, industry benchmarks, third-party valuations. This takes personal ego and emotion out of the equation. It's no longer about what *you* want versus what *they* want; it's about what is fair and standard in the industry.

Chapter Takeaway

Negotiation is not a dark art reserved for master manipulators. It is a core leadership skill—a structured process of principled, creative problem-solving. By preparing diligently, detaching from personal discomfort, and focusing on collaborative solutions, a leader can turn potentially adversarial encounters into powerful win-win outcomes that strengthen their business and their relationships.

Try This: The Pre-Negotiation Battle Plan

Never walk into a negotiation unprepared. Before any significant discussion, take 10 minutes to answer these questions in a notebook. This simple act of preparation will give you immense clarity and confidence.

1. **My Ideal Outcome:** What does a "grand slam" win look like for me in this negotiation?
2. **My Walk-Away Point:** What is the absolute minimum I will accept before I politely walk away from the deal? (Be specific: a price, a deadline, a specific term).
3. **Their Likely Interest:** Beyond their stated "position," what do I think the other party *truly* needs to get out of this deal? (e.g., To look good for their boss, to reduce their personal risk, to get a quick and easy solution).
4. **My Plan B (BATNA):** If this negotiation completely fails, what is my Best Alternative to a Negotiated Agreement? What will I do instead?

Chapter 22

From Idea to Invoice: The Leader's Innovation Playbook

Every leader dreams of creating the "next big thing." We all have ideas that we scribble on napkins or mull over in the shower—the game-changing product, the revolutionary service, the disruptive app.

The problem is, most of these brilliant ideas fail. They fail not because the idea was bad, but because the process was broken. The leader falls in love with their own clever solution, spends a year and a fortune building it in secret, and then unveils it to a market that shrugs and says, "...but I don't have that problem." They've just invented a revolutionary new typewriter in the age of the internet.

Innovation isn't a lightning strike of genius. It's not a mystical art. It is a disciplined, scientific process for turning a promising idea into a profitable reality. Your job as a leader is to build and run that process.

Phase 1: The Problem Lab (Fall in Love with the Problem, Not Your Solution)

This is the most critical and most frequently skipped phase. Before you ever think about a product, you must become a world-class expert on a *problem*—a real, painful, and urgent problem that a specific group of customers has.

- **Get Out of the Building:** Your best ideas are not inside your office walls. They are out in the world with your potential customers. Go talk to them. Watch them work. Ask about their frustrations, their goals, and the clunky "workarounds" they've invented to solve their problems.
- **Listen for the Pain:** Don't ask, "Would you buy a product that does X?" They will almost always say yes, because it's polite and hypothetical. Instead, ask about their current struggles: "What is the most frustrating part of your workday?" "What takes up the most time for the least reward?" "What do you wish you could just wave a magic wand and fix?"
- **Form a Testable Hypothesis:** The output of this phase is not a product spec; it's a simple, clear hypothesis. It looks like this: *"We believe [this specific customer group] struggles with [this specific, painful problem], and would pay for a solution that provides [this specific, measurable value]."*

Phase 2: The Workshop (Build a Skateboard, Not a Car)

Once you have a hypothesis, the temptation is to build the perfect, feature-packed solution. Resist this urge. Your goal now is to create a **Minimum Viable Product (MVP).**

The MVP is the smallest, simplest, cheapest version of your product that you can create to test your core hypothesis. It's not about building a car by starting with a tire, then an axle, then a chassis. That's pointless. It's about building a skateboard.

A skateboard isn't a car, but it solves the fundamental problem: "I need to get from Point A to Point B faster than walking." It allows you to test your core assumption with minimal investment. If people love the skateboard, you can then build a scooter. If they love the scooter, you can build a bicycle. Each step is a complete product that delivers value and, most importantly, generates learning.

Phase 3: The Proving Ground (From MVP to Validated Learning)

Now it's time to put your skateboard in front of real users—ideally, the same people you interviewed in Phase 1. Your goal is not to hear them say, "I like it." Your goal is to measure their *behavior*.

- **Do they use it?** Do they actually log in and try it out?
- **Do they come back?** One-time usage is a curiosity. Repeat usage is a signal of real value.
- **Would they pay for it?** This is the ultimate test. Even asking for a nominal amount, like $5, separates the polite enthusiasts from the serious customers.

This is the **Build-Measure-Learn** loop. You build the MVP. You measure the user behavior. You learn from the results. Then you use that learning to build the next version (the scooter) and repeat the cycle. This is where you decide whether to **pivot** (change your direction based on what you learned) or **persevere** (double down because your hypothesis is being proven correct).

Phase 4: The Launchpad (From Validated Product to Invoice)

Once you have iterated your way to a product that people are using, loving, and willing to pay for, it is finally time to scale. This is your Go-to-Market strategy, and it is not the time to "throw it over the wall" to your marketing and sales teams. They should have been involved all along.

Your launch plan is a final checklist:

- **Pricing:** What is the business model? (Subscription, one-time purchase, etc.)
- **Messaging:** What is the core story you are telling about the problem you solve? (See Chapter 5)

- **Channels:** Where will you reach your target customers? (See Chapter 13)
- **Sales & Support Readiness:** Is your sales team trained to sell it? Is your support team ready to handle inquiries?

This systematic process turns innovation from a high-stakes gamble into a series of calculated, low-cost experiments. It allows you to build solutions that the market wants.

Case Study: From a Costly Problem to a Custom Solution

The "Before" State (The Problem): I began working with a large association that hosted a major social event twice a year. To manage it, they were leasing a costly software solution, with annual support and licensing fees exceeding $30,000. Worse, this expensive system didn't even meet all of their requirements, forcing their staff to rely on clunky workarounds.

The Key Actions (The Process): After listening to their frustrations, my company formed a hypothesis: for slightly more than their *current one-year investment*, we could build them a *completely custom solution* that they would own forever. Our MVP was a beta version of the software that we let their team test internally. This allowed them to see if it met their core requirements before we launched it to their thousands of members. During this testing phase—our "Build-Measure-Learn" loop—we discovered additional, high-value features that we could add for very little extra cost, making the final product even better.

The "After" State (The Result): The final product has been a massive success. It has not only saved the association hundreds of thousands of dollars in leasing fees over the years but has also solved more problems than we initially scoped. The easy-to-use interface allows their members to submit data and make payments online seamlessly. It also includes a custom export feature that provides data for a print supplement that accompanies the event. The organization's ongoing annual cost to run this custom system is now typically less than $1,000, compared to the $30,000+ they were paying before.

Chapter Takeaway

Innovation isn't magic; it's a method. It's the discipline of identifying real-world problems, the humility to test your assumptions with small-scale experiments, and the wisdom to listen to customer behavior over your own biases. As a leader, your job isn't to be the sole genius with all the best ideas. Your job is to build and run the system that allows the best ideas—wherever they come from—to be discovered, tested, and brought to life.

Try This: The "Is This a Real Idea?" Litmus Test

Before you or your team get too excited about a "brilliant" new idea, run it through this quick, 3-question litmus test to see if it has real potential or if it's just a solution in search of a problem.

1. **The Problem Question:** Can I clearly and simply describe the specific, painful problem this idea solves for a specific group of people? (If you can't name the pain, the idea is just a hobby).
2. **The Evidence Question:** What evidence do we have that people are *already* trying to solve this problem? (Look for clunky workarounds, Google searches, forum complaints. If no one is trying to solve it, it might not be a real problem).

3. **The MVP Question:** What is the absolute smallest, cheapest, and fastest way we could build something to test if people would actually use our proposed solution? (Think skateboard, not car).

Chapter 23

Bringing It All Together: The Path of the Business Jedi

Padawan, listen well.

You have journeyed through the core disciplines of the modern business Force. You've studied the wisdom of **Leadership**, which provides the vision and moral compass. You've explored the subtle influence of **Marketing**, which reaches out across the galaxy to connect with and attract the right people. And you've honed the decisive skill of **Sales**, which turns interest into commitment.

Many business leaders master one of these, or dabble in all three. But true mastery doesn't lie in wielding just one saber. It's in uniting these three pillars of the Force. When leadership, marketing, and sales align, your business becomes a well-tuned starship: agile, powerful, and ready to jump to lightspeed.

Knowledge is not enough. Now, you must act. This is your guide to creating the clear, actionable battle plan that turns theory into results. This is your Jedi Code.

The Jedi Code: A Leader's Action Plan

A goal without a plan is just a wish. This framework turns your grand vision into a series of concrete steps, ensuring your entire team knows the mission and how to execute it.

Principle I: Define Your Quest (Set Clear, Measurable Goals) A Jedi doesn't just wander the galaxy hoping for adventure. They have a clear objective. Stop using vague ideas like "we want to improve sales." Get specific.

- **The Goal:** "We will increase sales by 20% in the next quarter."
- **The Breakdown:** That big goal is now broken into smaller, manageable tasks. The marketing team's quest is to generate 500 qualified leads. The sales team's quest is to close 50 deals. Now everyone knows exactly what success looks like and what is expected of them.

Principle II: Assemble Your Resources (The Right Tools and Team) A Jedi is only as good as their connection to the Force and the reliability of their lightsaber. Before you launch your quest, take stock of your resources.

- **Tools & Money:** Do you need new marketing software? A bigger ad budget? Does the plan fit the reality of your finances?
- **People & Skills:** Is your team trained to use these tools effectively? Does your sales team know the new product inside and out? Investing in training *before* you start is crucial. A well-

trained team works faster, makes fewer mistakes, and feels more confident and motivated.

Principle III: Chart Your Course (Timelines and Milestones) You wouldn't fly into an asteroid field without a map. Break down your quest into a clear timeline with specific deadlines and milestones.

- **Timelines** keep everyone focused and create a sense of urgency.
- **Milestones** are the mini-goals along the way that let you track progress and celebrate small wins. If your Q3 goal is a 20% sales increase, your first milestone might be a 5% increase in the first month. Hitting it builds momentum. Missing it gives you an early warning that you need to adjust your course.

Principle IV: Trust the Team, Track the Mission (Accountability and Feedback) A Jedi Master guides their apprentices but trusts them to execute their own missions.

- **Create Ownership:** Assign specific tasks to individuals or small groups. This creates accountability and ensures everyone knows their role. Use a shared project management tool so the entire team can see the plan, track their tasks, and see how their work fits into the bigger picture.
- **Communicate Clearly and Constantly:** Hold a kickoff meeting to discuss the plan in detail and answer all questions. Then, use regular check-ins to monitor progress, not to micromanage.
- **Use Feedback to Improve:** The plan is not set in stone. After a milestone—or a setback—gather the team. What worked? What didn't? What did we learn? Listening to your team's feedback makes them feel valued and makes your next plan even stronger.

Chapter Takeaway

True mastery in business doesn't lie in wielding just the saber of sales, the force of marketing, or the wisdom of leadership alone—it's in uniting them. When these disciplines align, your business becomes a well-tuned starship: agile, powerful, and ready to jump to light speed. So train in all three. Integrate. Lead. Sell. Market. Do this, and a business Jedi you shall become.

Chapter 24

The Leader as Athlete: Your Growth Regimen

Some leaders think their work is all "game day." They show up, make calls, and react to whatever comes their way. But the truly great leaders know that elite performance isn't just about what you do during the game; it's about how you train when no one is watching.

Think of yourself as a professional athlete. Your career is the sport. Your leadership is your skill. An athlete wouldn't dream of competing without a rigorous training plan, a healthy diet, and a commitment to understanding their own performance. Why should you?

This chapter is your personal training regimen. It's about moving from a reactive manager to a proactive "leadership athlete," one who is deliberately and consistently working on their own growth.

The Film Room: The Discipline of Self-Reflection

Every pro athlete spends hours in the film room, reviewing past plays to see what worked, what didn't, and where they can improve. This is your practice of self-reflection.

- **The Daily Journal:** Dedicate 15 minutes each morning or evening. Don't just list what you did; analyze it. "Why did that meeting go so well?" "What could I have done differently to support my team on that tough project?" This is where you spot the patterns in your own performance.
- **The Post-Campaign Debrief:** After every major marketing campaign or sales initiative, hold a debriefing session. Look at the metrics, but also ask your team for their honest feedback on your leadership during the process.
- **The One-on-One Feedback Session:** Schedule regular, informal check-ins with your team members and explicitly ask them for feedback on your leadership style. Questions like, "What is one thing I could start doing to better support you?" or "What is one thing I should stop doing?" will provide invaluable, unfiltered insights.

The Holistic Athlete: Training Your Body, Spirit, and Mind

Elite athletes know that performance isn't just about skills; it's about the whole person. To avoid burnout and lead with clarity and energy, you must train the "trinity" of your own well-being.

- **Train Your Body:** This is the foundation. You can't lead effectively if you're physically drained. This means prioritizing sleep, maintaining proper nutrition, and engaging in regular exercise. Your physical health directly fuels your mental resilience and stamina.

- **Train Your Spirit:** This is about finding your inner calm and purpose. For some, it's mindfulness or meditation; for others, it's spending time in nature or with family. This practice fosters the mental stillness required to handle stress, make thoughtful decisions, and lead with empathy instead of reactivity.
- **Train Your Mind:** Your brain is a muscle. You must actively work it out. Read a leadership book every month. Attend a workshop or seminar. Seek out a mentor who can challenge your thinking. Join a networking group to learn from the experiences of other leaders. Continuous learning broadens your perspective and keeps your strategic skills sharp.

Your Personal Growth "Workout Plan"

Here is a list of ongoing activities to incorporate into your leadership training regimen.

- Dedicate 15 minutes each morning to journaling.
- Schedule weekly one-on-one meetings to solicit feedback.
- Read one leadership book or a handful of insightful articles each month.
- Seek a mentor who can provide guidance and challenge your style.
- Join a leadership networking or peer group.
- Engage in 5-10 minutes of mindfulness or meditation daily.

Chapter Takeaway (for Growth as a Leader)

Great leadership isn't a title you're given; it's a craft you hone. By adopting the mindset of a professional athlete—committing to daily training, reviewing your performance, and nurturing your mind, body, and spirit—you build the strength, resilience, and wisdom to not just play the game, but to change it.

Try This: The Weekly "Coach's Review"

At the end of each week, take 10 minutes to be your own leadership coach. This isn't about criticizing yourself; it's about identifying opportunities for growth, just like an athlete reviewing game tape. Ask yourself these three questions:

1. **The "Win" Reel:** What was my single biggest leadership "win" this week? (e.g., I handled a difficult conversation well, I empowered a team member successfully, I stayed calm under pressure). How can I replicate that?
2. **The "Learning" Reel:** What was one moment this week where I could have been a better leader? (e.g., I interrupted someone in a meeting, I didn't give clear enough direction, I avoided a tough conversation). What will I do differently next time?
3. **The "Energy" Meter:** On a scale of 1-10, what was my energy and focus level this week? What one thing can I do next week to protect or recharge my energy?

Chapter 25

The Leader's Armor: Managing the Inevitable Stress of Command

Leadership is a contact sport. Every day, you face a barrage of demands, challenges, and unexpected crises. But when we talk about stress, we often make the mistake of thinking it only comes from being overworked. The truth is, the most toxic forms of stress are often far more subtle.

I learned this early in my corporate career. I had applied for a promotion in the advertising department, and while I didn't get it, my supervisor saw potential in me and suggested a different path: a junior programmer role. I was excited. I dove into the training, eager to learn a new skill and contribute.

But I quickly discovered the job had very little to do with programming. My real, unspoken task was to spy on and report on a senior programmer. This individual held specialized knowledge that no one else on the team had, and management, in a stunning display of dysfunction, chose suspicion over collaboration.

For weeks, I was a ghost in the machine. I was given no direction, little to no instruction, and no real tasks. I would sit at my desk all day in a state of limbo, trapped in an ethically compromised position with no clear purpose.

The stress I felt during that time wasn't burnout from a heavy workload. It was the crushing weight of feeling useless. It was the defeat that came from a complete lack of purpose. And it was the constant, low-grade fear of simply "waiting for the inevitable," knowing I was in an untenable situation.

That experience taught me that a leader's most significant responsibility in managing stress is not just about workloads; it's about providing clarity, purpose, and psychological safety. A toxic environment of uncertainty and mistrust will break a team faster than any heavy project ever could.

Your effectiveness as a leader is directly tied to your ability to manage stress and create an environment that protects your team from its adverse effects. This chapter is about how to forge your armor.

Know Your Armor's Weak Points: Recognizing Stress

Before you can defend against stress, you have to be self-aware enough to know when you're under attack. The signs are often subtle at first.

- **Irritability:** Are you snapping at people over small things?
- **Fatigue:** Do you feel tired all the time, even after a full night's sleep?
- **Lack of Focus:** Are you having trouble concentrating on a single task or making a clear decision?

Being mindful of these symptoms in yourself is the first, critical step. Acknowledging "I am feeling overwhelmed right now" is a sign of strength, not weakness.

Forging Your Armor: The Three Layers of Protection

Resilience isn't something you're born with; it's something you build. Here are three layers of "armor" to cultivate.

- **Layer 1: The Mindful Shield (Mental Practices):** This is your inner defense.
    - **Deep Breathing:** When you feel pressure mounting, take 60 seconds. Inhale slowly through your nose, hold, and exhale slowly through your mouth. It's a physiological reset button.
    - **Mindfulness:** Practice paying attention to the present moment without judgment. This can be through meditation apps or simply by taking a moment to notice your thoughts without getting carried away by them.
    - **Positive Affirmations:** Start your day by reminding yourself of your strengths and achievements. This isn't cheesy; it's about consciously setting a confident, resilient tone for the day.

- **Layer 2: The Structured Gauntlets (Practical Habits):** This is how you control your environment.
    - **Time Management:** Use lists and planners to prioritize your most important tasks. A clear plan reduces the feeling of being overwhelmed.
    - **Set Boundaries:** Learn to say "no" to non-essential demands. Block out time in your calendar for focused work and protect it ruthlessly. Take real breaks during the day to step away and recharge.
    - **Physical Activity:** Regular exercise is one of the most powerful stress reducers available. A walk at lunch or a morning workout improves mood and energy levels.
- **Layer 3: The Supporting Garrison (External Support):** No one fights alone.
    - **Mentors and Colleagues:** Having a trusted mentor or peer to talk to provides an essential outlet and a fresh perspective on your challenges.
    - **Your Team:** When you foster a healthy work environment where your team can also manage their stress, it reduces the overall pressure on you. Implement workshops on stress relief or encourage flexible schedules.

When you prioritize your own well-being, you're not just helping yourself. You are modeling the behavior that creates a healthier, more resilient, and more productive environment for everyone.

Final Takeaway

Running a business is an exciting expedition, not a sprint. Every challenge is an opportunity in disguise. This book is your toolkit, packed with practical strategies to help you not just survive the journey but thrive along the way. With a clear plan as your compass and confidence in your vision, you are well-equipped to chart a course toward success. The best is yet to come. You will be a truly great leader.

GOOD LUCK!!!

About the Author

Meet Michael Hutchinson—AKA Hutch

Michael Hutchinson, MBA—or as his friends (and probably a few lucky clients) call him, Hutch—is not your typical business consultant. He's a sales, marketing, and strategy ninja who thrives on helping businesses succeed… or at least stop making the same mistakes on repeat. He blazed through his MBA in just four months, proving he can absorb and apply complex business concepts faster than most people decide what to watch on Netflix.

A Natural Teacher & Problem-Solving Prodigy

By 22, Hutch was already teaching college classes on web design, coding, and print design. That's right—while most people his age were still figuring out their careers, he was at the front of the room explaining CSS and design principles. His ability to break down complex topics in a way that's clear, logical, and even a little fun is one of his core strengths.

This knack for clarity goes beyond the classroom. Hutch has a sixth sense for untangling business knots. Whether it's a flawed strategy, a failing marketing campaign, or a website that loads at the speed of a tortoise, he can diagnose the problem and get it fixed. But his real gift is untangling the human knots—getting teams to communicate effectively, build meaningful connections, and feel like they've learned something valuable in the process.

Award-Winning Marketing Guru

When it comes to marketing, Hutch has the hardware to back up the hype. He's won multiple awards from the American Marketing Association (AMA), pro ving his strategies don't just sound good on paper—they deliver real-world results. He even served on the board for the AMA's Oklahoma City chapter, helping shape the local marketing scene and sharing his expertise with fellow professionals.

A Heart for the Community

When he's not busy solving business puzzles, Hutch is focused on giving back. He serves on the board for two incredible children's charities—**Vizavance**, which provides free vision screenings for children, and **The Toby Keith Foundation**, which supports families battling pediatric cancer. For Hutch, making a difference in young lives is just as important as making businesses thrive.

Need a Business Lifeline?

If you're looking for someone who can diagnose your business woes, craft a winning strategy, and make you laugh while doing it, Hutch is your guy. He's also the CEO and a managing partner at Directing Design, Inc., where he and his team help brands cut through the noise and build digital experiences that actually work. To see what they're about, check out their work at directingdesign.com or connect with Hutch on LinkedIn: https://www.linkedin.com/in/hutchee/.

www.ingramcontent.com/pod-product-compliance
Lightning Source LLC
LaVergne TN
LVHW010946110826
845149LV00015B/3234